LOSING SARAH

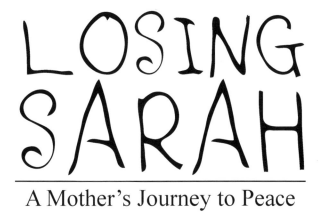

LOSING SARAH

A Mother's Journey to Peace

LORRENE DESBIEN

authorHOUSE®

AuthorHouse™
1663 Liberty Drive
Bloomington, IN 47403
www.authorhouse.com
Phone: 1-800-839-8640

Published by AuthorHouse   10/26/2012

ISBN: 978-1-4772-8607-4 (sc)
ISBN: 978-1-4772-8606-7 (e)

Library of Congress Control Number: 2012920481

September 24

Dear friends,

It is with a heavy heart that I tell you of the passing of our sweet Sarah. When she was born, they whisked her away from me because she was so sick. And once again she has been whisked away. Last night, I texted her at 9:11 and told her to buckle up. At 9:12 she texted me and told me that she was buckled and LOL. About thirty minutes later, I texted her to tell her that I loved her. It was at about that same time that she left me.

She and two friends were southbound on I-35 when the tire came untreaded. The rear of the car swung around and hit a pole of some kind, killing her instantly. Fortunately, the other two people in the car were not seriously injured. Ironically, it was very near Cimarron Turnpike, which is the highway on which her grandfather passed away. She passed away in the same month as her grandfather twenty-two years ago. She also passed away on the anniversary of her great-grandmother Lillie's death.

I want you to know that the young man driving the car came to my house today with his parents to face us. I think this was incredibly brave. We hold no grudges whatsoever against him, and we want our friends to lift him up in prayer and love and grace, as Sarah would have expected. He is crushed.

Sarah's last day of life was one of the best she had ever had. She and several friends got ready for Spirit Day in my classroom. She had forgotten to put her jeans in the dryer the night before, so we had to put them in the locker room dryer (which was hilarious to her). Her friend fixed her hair, and she was so excited to be having a great hair day. It was homecoming, so there was a lot of free time. She came into my classroom every once in a while. The little kids loved her and Emily [one of my other daughters], and they loved Friday because Sarah colored with them, pushed them on the swing, and tasted imaginary pies.

After school, she spent some time with friends and then worked at the concession stand for the game in my place, as I was sick. After the game, she and Emily met Larry and me at the car, and we gave them money. As they walked away, I said, "Good choices, girls." They both laughed and said, "Okay!"

Sarah ran across the street. She had denim shorts on her long legs and a football jersey. Her hair was floating in the breeze, and there was a headlight shining on her. I thought she never looked more beautiful. She told me she loved me, and she was gone.

Larry and I went to Walmart, and after we got home, there was a knock on the door. I opened it and there stood the highway patrol. I screamed for Larry and ran away.

Peace and grace be yours in abundance.

[We would learn much later that she was not killed instantly but lived for fifty minutes.]

Texts from that night

On the way to Lamont for the football game, I sent all the pictures that had been taken Friday at Spirit Day on my phone to the parents of my students.

8:00: I texted Emily, "I am by the cafeteria," meaning I was sitting on the end of the football field nearest the cafeteria. She had a hard time hearing me when she called to ask where I was, so I texted her back.

8:17: I texted Sarah to say, "Thank you so much for working." She was working in the concession stand for me.

9:05: after the game being called at half time on the mercy rule (we were forty-five points ahead), I texted Connor's mom, "Good Job, Uncle Connor!" Connor is the uncle of one of my students, and they love him so much.

9:07: I texted, "New thing—Raspberry Dr. Pepper. OMG—you have got to try it," to Sarah and Emily

9:09: Sarah said, "Oh Gosh. Lol."

9:10: I texted Caroline [my other daughter], "did you get all moved?" She was moving into a different house.

9:11: I texted Sarah, "Are you buckled?"

9:12: Sarah texted me, "yes lol."

9:43: I texted Emily and Sarah, "Love you."

I had tried to call Emily, and at 10:18 she texted me, "I'm in the place. lol." I took this to mean that she couldn't hear at that time because of all the noise.

10:20: I texted Emily, "Dance? Having fun?""

10:21: Emily's response was, "Yeah and I'm just really tired."

10:22: Me to Emily: "I didn't think about how to get u home tomorrow."

10:23: Emily: "Oh . . . uh . . . me neither."

Here I have purposely left out sis texts between Emily and me, discussing a boy she is interested in.

Around this time the highway patrol came, and I made a screaming phone call to my mother. I do not remember what I said or she said, except screaming that she was gone. I called Caroline. I called my Aunt Lisa. Then I tried to call my dearest friend, Shelly Braden, and it rolled to her answering machine. Then I called LeaAnne Shelton, and she answered. I tried to call Merle Ann and couldn't dial. I don't remember much of the conversations or what happened after that. I just remember them being here.

11:10: "Thanks for all those great pics!!! OMG!!!" This was from Barbara Kirby, thanking me for the pictures I had sent of Sarah, Connor, and Cooper. (At this time I called her, but am not sure exactly what I said. I basically told her and asked her help me get Emily home.)

9/24: Early morning hours after learning we had lost Sarah. We sent out this e-mail to many friends: "Please pray for us, we were just informed that we lost our Sarah in a car accident tonight."

September 24, Evening There are a few updates to give you:

Sarah looks as beautiful as always. There is not a scratch on her. [I would later learn that there were several external injuries that were covered up.] We are so relieved that we will be able to have an open casket so that everyone can see how beautiful she is one more time.

Emily, Larry, and I went to The Buckle [Sarah's favorite store] to purchase the clothing that she will be buried in. When the lady asked me if she could help me, all I could say was she wore a 3 extra-long and that I wanted that size in a skinny jean. I was weeping, and so was Emily. The girl working found us the perfect pair of jeans; they had angel wings on the pocket. Emily also bought a pair to match. Emily then did the most unselfish and huge thing ever: she took over the selection of the burial clothes for her sister, while Larry and I followed her around blindly.

She chose a green, purple, and brown plaid with a green undershirt and a purple undershirt. She also chose the jewelry. I want you to know that the service was incredible, with the girl racing around the store to help Emily complete this sad task. Emily purchased a purple shirt to wear with her jeans for the funeral and said that she will wear this outfit every Wednesday to remember her sister. At the end of the shopping, I found three rings with purple stones. I bought one for each of my girls. It will be the last time I purchase three of anything for my girls.

Caroline will be taking Baylee to The Buckle tomorrow to purchase their outfits. Caroline is a trooper also. She chose the casket spray and chose purple mums and white lilies. She has tried to be as helpful as always. She is angry and hurt.

Michael called me this evening and forwarded a picture of Sarah. Trenton and Kisen were here this evening. They are getting tats with her name. They have it designed and have made the commitment that if I chose to get a tattoo, they would pay for it. What loving young men.

We have confirmed with our list of pallbearers. They are Kisen Sharp, Trenton Anderson, Mitchell Hadley, Blake Holmes, Robert Neumayer, and Tyler Jeffries. While we have not confirmed our list of honorary pallbearers, we know that the list will include Jacob "Pillsbury" Massey and the DCLA football team and coaching staff.

Ronnie will not be able to come home. While we have very different jobs, we both are dedicated to service to others and sometimes that commitment imposes on our family time.

We are overwhelmed by the outpouring of love and prayers. We had no idea that we had so many friends. Our bucket of love is filled with your kind acts, which is great, because we keep crying it empty.

September 24

The sunset was beautiful tonight. People from southern Texas all the way up to western Kansas sent us messages that they saw it. Larry and I went and stood in the middle of the street and watched it. It was breathtaking.

September 25

We are all up and have had showers this morning. We were all able to get some sleep. It had been a lifetime since we left for school on homecoming morning for what was to be the best day of Sarah's life. She was so happy, and there were so many, many beautiful pictures taken of her.

Someone brought me pretty sunflowers that he had picked himself. Larry and I had talked about the sunflowers that were growing on the way to the football game at Lamont. When Larry saw the sunflowers, he mentioned seeing them Friday night, and I couldn't believe that it had been less than twenty-four hours since we had that conversation. That was a whole lifetime ago. Several times Sarah commented about what a great hair day she was having. Larry had said several times what a beautiful night it was, and he had pointed out Venus in the evening sky. On the way home, I leaned to the window and looked at the stars. We both just kept commenting about what a beautiful night it was.

We are going to the funeral home today at two to choose between the two purple caskets. The chosen one will then be overnighted, as she will be readied to say good-bye to her friends. We have decided that I will see her. I struggled with this decision, because it seems almost too much to bear. But Mom says that she looks so peaceful and almost has a smile.

We have confirmation that Mike Anderson will be an honorary pall bearer. Sarah dated Mike's son, Trenton, for over a year. Even though they broke up quite some time ago, Trenton was still a frequent visitor to our home. She called Mike the Hot Old Guy.

We were all able to talk to Ronnie today. Sarah will be laid to rest with her Uncle Ronnie's dog tags. She would really dig that—she wanted to be in the army, but knew her health would never let her. When dad died twenty-two years ago this month; Ronnie was only seventeen, but he was left to be the man of the family. Now, from a half a world away, he is holding our family together. Dad would be proud of the job he has done.

We have been amazed at the diversity of young people coming to our home. Kids with all societal labels and from all cultural backgrounds have filled our home with light and noise at a time when we can't stand the quiet and darkness. Sarah hated labels and loved passionately people from all walks. She had ability far beyond her years and experience to see past all the crap to get to the heart of who someone was. We always laughed, because when she would come dragging some teenager home, I would ask, "Are you a drug dealer?" and if it was a boy, "Do you paint your fingernails black?" Larry would occasionally come into the living room, look onto the front porch, where she loved to hang, and say, "Now, who is this kid? I have never seen them before." And I would look out, and there would be some random kid on my front porch that I had never laid eyes on. These "random kids" have just blessed and blessed us in the last hours.

Michael, the driver of the car, called last night and asked if he could send us a picture that Sarah had sent him just a few minutes before the accident. It is beautiful. I think he has a long row to hoe. His mama had to support him physically yesterday. He just shook when Larry and I held him.

Larry broke down and cried last night when he was thanking my friends who were here first. He said that the first thirty minutes until they got here were really bad, because he didn't know what to do for me, because I was just lying in the backyard screaming. And then these women showed up and were able to help.

I just really don't remember a lot about that time. I remember throwing my phone at the highway patrolman. I remember running away and not being the one he told. I remember coming back into the living and screaming, "Is she gone?" And Larry just turning to me and nodding. I remember the highway patrolman asking if this was the "Ray" residence. At some point I remember my mom holding my face in the backyard and saying my name and saying, "Oh, my baby, my baby, what can I do for you?" I remember begging Lisa not to tell Emily yet. I knew that once Emily knew, it was real.

It is terrible, and it is beautiful. The last hours have been a true celebration of her life and who she was. We are amazed at the love and grace that we have been filled with. Larry commented last night, on our way to pick out her clothes, that we have really good friends.

Saying that we love you just isn't enough, so I will leave you for now by telling you this: Several years ago, I walked into a room full of teachers, and the principal announced that I would be returning the following year as assistant principal. The teachers at that school cheered and clapped. I said at that time that everyone, at some point in their life, should stand in a room and have the people they love and respect applaud them. I wish for you that you someday know the love of your friends and family as we now know. We knew that we had good folks in our life, but we never knew the scale of the love that people have for us. The Facebook comments and messages, the calls, the visits, the people filling our home, it is all beautiful and perfect—just like you.

Peace and grace be yours in abundance.

Sarah's Obituary

On a frigid morning, January 4, 1995, Sarah Virginia Ray danced her way into our life. When she was born, she was whisked away because she was so sick. On September 23, 2011, she was once again whisked away from us. Sarah was a very good baby who seldom cried. She had a soft voice and spoke very quickly and slurred. She couldn't say her big sister's name and called her Bludderline.

From the time that she was an infant, she rocked herself. When she was big enough to kick her leg, she rocked herself in her car seat and would sit up and rock so hard in her crib that she would move it away from the wall. Her rocking chair sits empty by her mother's piano, having been rocked in by Sarah for the last time, the night before she left us.

Several years ago, Larry Desbien took Sarah's mom and all three girls on a date. The girls loved him instantly, and he promised that he would be a positive influence in their lives. After returning from their honeymoon, Sarah, ever the analyzer and actionist, sat Larry down and asked if she could call him Dad. He kept his promise to her and was always fair and patient, taking her on trips and to concerts and art exhibits and IMAX movies.

Sarah grew up in Blackwell and Ponca City and loved people of all shapes, sizes, colors, and backgrounds. She was an advocate against social labels and refused to allow them to determine whether or not she was going to love a person. And she didn't just like people, she loved them fiercely.

She loved the nighttime, music, the army, her middle name, her grandmother, dancing, apples, driving, and purple. She loathed society, the government, prejudice, therapy, weird flavored ice cream (which included anything but chocolate), and snitches. She collected quotes, photographs, and the hearts of all who stumbled across her.

She and her sisters went to several schools following her mother's teaching career that included Kaw City and McCord. In Ponca City, she attended East and West. In Blackwell she attended Washington Center, Huston Center, Blackwell Middle School, and Blackwell High School. Sarah was currently a junior at DCLA High School.

Never one to be merely an onlooker at life, Sarah actively sought out new experiences. She had been in 4-H and FFA while in Blackwell and had the opportunity to show pigs, thanks to her sister's father, Robert Neumayer. She was in band and played the flute.

She had played softball, serving her various teams as pitcher and catcher. After taking a line drive to the face that left her unconscious, she returned to the mound the following night after informing her coach that if she waited, she might not do it again at all. Typical Sarah, looking the fear in the face and telling it, "No sir, not today will you beat me."

She spoke fluent Spanish and was learning to play the guitar. She had recently expressed an interest in learning the piano. She was an avid writer and had won awards for her prose. She and her mother had been discussing an essay that she was currently writing on their morning drives to Lamont.

From the day that Sarah was born, she had an old soul and was a full-time world observer, brewer, and mulling-over-er of deep thoughts, creative ideas, and big problems. Sarah struggled with depression and often felt very doubtful of her own worth. After years of therapy, Sarah had found a very sacred place to live her last days. Six weeks before her death, her mother started teaching at Lamont and told Sarah, "This is the place for us. Please come and look at it." Sarah came to the school and visited with Michael Thompson, the principal, who was able to "sell" it to her. She started the next day. It was a magical and beautiful time for her as the students and adults welcomed her with open arms and hearts.

The night before she died, she and her mother went on a midnight excursion in which Sarah learned to drive the standard. At the beginning she said that it was the worst experience ever. As they turned on to her street, Sarah said, "Can you believe how I am rocking it?" The two of them pulled out the hideaway couch and sat up until 3:00 a.m. talking.

The last day of her life was the most beautiful and perfect day ever. That morning as she stood in the bathroom, her mom took a quiet moment to hug her from behind as Sarah leaned her head on her mom's cheek. No words—just love. As they were leaving the house, Sarah's mom grabbed a CD and popped in the player in the car. Without knowing it, her mom had picked up the CD that Sarah had recently been listening to. Sarah asked for the song about "all the people," and her mom put it on—"Imagine" by John Lennon (as sung by Eva Cassidy). They listened to it several times with Sarah singing.

Also on the drive to school they discussed an essay Sarah was working on once again, and Emily and Sarah discussed how they were going to wear their hair. Several friends got ready for school in her mother's prekindergarten classroom, as had become the norm. She was having a great hair day. Because it was homecoming, she had free time and took the opportunity to come to her mother's classroom several times to hang out with the kids. That evening at the football game, Sarah worked in the concession stand in place of her mother, who was ill. She had the opportunity to spread the miracle that was Sarah to many people that night. After the game she and Emily came to the car to touch base with their parents, as they had plans for the rest of the night. She had on a football jersey and denim shorts, and her hair was waving in the wind. As she ran across the street, there was a headlight shining on her. She yelled, "Love you!" She never looked more beautiful, and then she was gone. She sent her love to the world one more time with the most beautiful purple sunset the following night.

Sarah will be celebrated at the Blackwell High School Auditorium at 2:00 p.m. on Wednesday, September 28, 2011. We ask that you wear purple. She will be laid to rest at the I.O.O.F. cemetery in Ponca City next to her grandfather. Casket bearers will be her special friends Kisen Sharp, Trenton Anderson, Robert Neumayer, her brother-in-law Mitchell Hadley, and cousins, Tyler Jeffries, and Blake Holmes. Honorary casket bearers will be the defending state champion DCLA Eagle football team: Jacob "Pillsbury" Massey, Mike Anderson, Bennett Shipley, Mariella Sanchez, Kayla Hillhouse, Kalli Alley, Kore Chapman, Austin Neufield, Michael Brown, Eric Simpson, Clint Arnold, and Kodi Burns. In addition, her teachers at DCLA who had created a magical place where she could finally find peace: Doug Sinor, Kelly Riddle, Kelly Ridgeway, Jared Johnson, Janice Wilkerson, Michael Thompson, Chad Hutchinson, and David Zachary.

She is survived by her heartbroken family, her parents, Larry and Lorrie Desbien, her sisters, Caroline Elizabeth Neumayer Hadley, Emily Jane Ray, Jennifer Suzanne Ray, and Chanda Prater, her brother, Justin Gene Ray, her brothers-in-law, Ben Prater and Mitchell Hadley, and her grandmother who was so precious to her, Virgie Holmes. She also loved and admired her special uncle, Capt. Ronnie Holmes Jr., a flight surgeon currently serving at FOB Sarana, Afghanistan. Biological father, Anthony Ray, and paternal grandparents, Ocie and Sue Ray.

Welcoming her to heaven are her grandfather, Ron Holmes Sr., and her grandmother, Charlotte Desbien.

Sarah lived a life that was accentuated by service to others. She wanted to follow her uncle into the army, but was not healthy enough. She struggled with a career choice that was right, until she heard about brothers who were making mission trips to Haiti. She then knew that she would do that kind of work. In that spirit, donations will be made to establish a fund to purchase shoes for children.

September 26

We went to the funeral home today to finalize the plans. When we got there, Karmen had just arrived in town with Blake and Baylee, so they met us there. It was such a relief that they had made it home safely.

We did not get a purple casket. Both were actually gray with a purple tint when the light hit them, and they were very shiny. They were also lined with pink, and she would not have liked that. We found a perfect wood casket that we thought looked like her, so after a phone call to Caroline and Emily, that is what we chose. We think that it will look good with the outfit that Emily chose and the spray that Caroline chose. As Larry and I were standing alone, I whispered to him, "How is this possible? How are we picking out a casket for our child?" He just whispered back, "I don't know," and rubbed my back.

We had to choose the stationary. They all looked very "funereally," and I hated them all, except one that kept catching my attention. I said I liked it, and everyone in the room—my BFF, my mom, my aunt, my sister-in-law, and my husband—all smiled and said they thought that would be best. That was the one we had all been drawn to.

Mom did Sarah's hair and got her ready. She does have an abrasion on her arm that mom says looks like angel wings, and her hair had to be fixed a certain way to cover some injuries. This was troubling to me, because we had been told there weren't any visibly injuries. I have not faced her yet. I will go tomorrow and spend some time with her before the viewing.

We have confirmed the following list of honorary casket bearers; we just kept thinking of people we love and who loved Sarah. The DCLA football team (who will be wearing purple wristbands in her honor Friday night), Jacob "Pillsbury" Massey, Mike Anderson (the Hot Old Guy), Bennet Shipley, Mariella Sanchez, Kayla Hillhouse, Kalli Alley, Kore Chapman, Austin Nuefield, Michael Brown, Clint Arnold (who she had a profound amount of respect for), Eric Simpson (who she hassled every chance she got), and her teachers at DCLA who provided a safe place for her to be Sarah: Doug Sinor, Kelly Riddle, Jared Johnson, Janice Wilkerson, Michael Thompson, Chad Hutchinson, David Zachery, and Kelly Ridgeway.

There will be lots of music and photographs and purple and tears.

I went through her backpack today and found several precious things: an essay about her family that she had written in Spanish; the compare-contrast essay we had been discussing last week on our rides to school; the ribbon she used as she decorated a shirt for her friend for Spirit Day; several purple notebooks; notes, test papers, and school work; her medications; her inhaler; a note with a tongue sticking out that someone had made; and jewelry—but no wallet, no driver's license, and no class ring. We are still looking for those, and they are not at the hospital.

Here are some incredible things that speak to the type of person my child was: Sarah struggled with depression and self-worth. We found a list that she had started that was a new writing idea for her: "50 Things I Love and 50 Things I Loathe." Even though I felt I was struggling as a parent, she had listed me on the "Things I Love" side. It broke my heart to see that on the "Things I Loathe" side, she had listed "Sarah." In the same pocket of the backpack, there was a torn dollar bill. I was going to throw it away one day and she stopped me, saying, "Mom, just because it is torn, doesn't mean it doesn't have value." I think she compared herself to that torn dollar . . . . She had also tagged me in a quote that said, "Her life improved drastically when she decided to break the rules and find beauty where she had been told there was none."

I have written her obituary. Tara made a beautiful set of letters spelling her name. Baylee has designed a special T-shirt. Friends have been e-mailing pictures and digging pictures out. It is such a blessing to remember and to see pictures that I had not seen before.

Again today my house was filled with kids, and my heart with such love. Our family is traveling to DCLA High School in the morning, where they will be having a moment of silence. It will occur at about 9:15 to give the seniors a chance to arrive. We will then be going to get Larry a purple tie, pick up Caroline and Baylee's outfits, get Larry a haircut, and meet with the pastor. After that I will go take her stuff; Granny will give her a squirt of her favorite perfume; and she will be ready.

Larry has had a very hard day today. He is very tired, and because he is a fixer, he is at a loss. He has cried with me several times today.

Caroline and Emily have cried a lifetime of tears today. They will forever have one third of a heart missing. Caroline is doing what she has always done and is comforting Emily at all times. Every time I see Caroline, she is doing something for Emily. Emily just lies on the couch; friends come and go, and she just lies there.

We did receive some news that eased my mind. We had been told that she was killed instantly, but we now know that she lived for about fifteen minutes after the accident. She was taken to Perry Hospital, where it was determined that there was no hope. The accident happened at 9:35. When I heard that she had passed away at 9:35, I was devastated. I had sent her a text at 9:43telling her that I loved her, and I was afraid that she didn't get it. Knowing that she lived for longer, leads me to believe that at least she was alive when I sent the text, even if she didn't read it.

Larry and I were in Walmart, and I felt compelled to pull out my cell phone and text her that. I was very upset, because she didn't get it before the accident. I am now certain that when I felt that urge to send her the text, it was her leaving me. No matter what the death certificate says, Sarah left me at 9:43.

Peace and grace be yours in abundance.

September 26

One other thing that I intended to include in my post and left out. It cannot wait until tomorrow: Blake (Ronnie's son) found a shirt of Sarah's at his house. He put it on the back of his pickup seat and Sarah is riding shotgun every day. She would dig that.

September 26

We went to DCLA today for a brief service for Sarah. The superintendent spoke very simple words with a profound message. He said to the kids, "I have no answers." He spoke to them about faith and knowing that he was going to see her again and that the kids could honor her by loving Emily and me. The band director, who is also a preacher, spoke and led us in prayer. I spoke. The kids are devastated. They have nowhere to go with this grief.

We then went down to my room where I was mauled to death with hugs. They asked some questions.

Cooper wanted to know, "Where is Sarah, 'cause I love her?" He always got the biggest kick out of saying, "Just Sarah and Emily," when I asked him who he loved. I would act a fool and have a fit, and he would laugh.

Cantrell, who is the imaginary pie maker, came up to me with no words and stroked my cheek, turned my head, and kissed my cheek. His mother had told him what had happened to Sarah. When he pulled away, he had tears in his eyes. Compassion is pretty typical of Cantrell. He sits by people who are crying and looks at them and pats them.

My class sang for my family. My sweet Alexis, who prayed for God to help her find a purple flower for her teacher, was not there.

Paeton wanted to know if I would be there tomorrow or the next day or the other one. "Why you not come to school no more?" he asked me.

We left my room and had a few more tears. We looked in her locker. Baylee was surprised that the lockers didn't have locks. I guess we forget how special this place is.

Emily does not want to be touched. She is still just lying on the couch quite a bit.

We did hear today that Sarah's dad will be attending her service. I want to make it very clear that even though there have been some hurt feelings, now is the time for grace and healing. We do not know the reasons behind the actions of others. Judging others does not define them; it defines us. So my expectation is that he be treated with respect and love and compassion.

We will be seeing Sarah at 3:00 p.m. today. Kisen is driving over to help get her room ready, and I think Trenton may be coming too. She will be receiving friends at five. I finished her canvases with quotes. I randomly chose several quotes. When they were done, Emily came in and said, "Mom, that was her favorite quote."

I think that those attending the service will be pleasantly surprised at it. It is going to be perfect, just like all of you. The only thing I have left to do is the slide show. I am pretty certain that I have found all the perfect pictures.

I found some of her writing today—two notebooks of it. There was one story about me in there. I also found a piece of paper that she must have written during one of her dark times that said, "NO MORE."

We did find her driver's license today. Still no class ring.

Peace and grace be yours in abundance.

September 26

Sarah is ready to receive friends.

September 27

The funniest thing, I just *died* laughing. I had a pretty ugly shower this morning—one of those sitting on the floor sobbing kind of showers. I did quite a bit of apologizing and asking Sarah to forgive me. Then I got out, dried off, and this memory happened: The girls and I were going somewhere and I had on white pants. Of course I can *rock* a pair of white pants, so I went in thinking I was looking fabulous. About halfway across the parking lot, Caroline says, "Hey, Mom, nice purple underwear." And I said, *"Why didn't you tell me before we left the house?!"* Sarah said, "Well, it wouldn't have been funny then." I was thinking about that as I went upstairs. I was digging through my drawer looking for a pair of underwear and felt around and pulled out what has to be the my last pair of clean underwear—they were the same exact pair of purple underwear I had been wearing on that silly day.

September 27

Mornings are the worst. I am not consciously thinking that I have to face a whole day without her, but I think my heart knows it. I am very thankful for the things to do each day.

I'm making little lists so that I can mark things off. There seems to be something good about marking things off. Today I have to buy a toothbrush. Sarah had grabbed the wrong one Friday morning and had thrown it in her purse, and I can't find another one. I have to find some purple toenail polish that isn't hideous. She and I always jousted about toenail polish color; she and Emily always wanted me to use some outrageous color like black or paint them all different colors like they did. I told her, "Ladies don't do that." She and Emily always wondered who made these rules. I told them I would look ridiculous; they said I would look fabulous.

We did go see her and get her chapel ready. Larry and I went in alone first, and the grief and panic when I looked at my child in her casket was almost more than I could bear. She is beautiful. It is all I can say. My mom did her hair and makeup, and it is perfect. How a grandmother has the strength to do that is beyond me.

When we saw her, I don't know what happened, but Mom and Larry and Karmen and the funeral home director helped me sit up and then stand up. While I was lying on the floor, I could hear my mom saying, "Oh my baby," and rubbing my face. I can't imagine what it would be like to lose your grandchild and then have to help your own child. I don't think she has time for her own grief.

I cannot articulate how amazed I am at the diversity of kids coming through that chapel and through our home. Kids that I had in class. Kids that were her friends. From all walks of life. Last night I met the famous Raul that she talked about frequently. Jake came over when he was leaving, I said, "Good-bye, you freak of nature." From being such a little boy, he has grown up into this amazing, strong, confident, and handsome young man. It is so strange to hug these boys that I had in second and third grade who are now taller than me. When I see the girls, it is so funny because I think, "Oh, she is wearing makeup now." They have no place to go with this pain.

There will be a candlelight vigil for Sarah at 7:15. We will be driving to Lamont by seven. We will then leave DCLA at 7:30 to go to Blackwell at eight. I am just overwhelmed by these young people and how precious and compassionate they are as they grapple with this very grown-up thing.

The driver of the car came to the house. Sarah had asked him to hold her money for her that night, and he brought it to us. She had been saving her money to get extensions, and she had all of her money with her. We had to have some of her hair cut (more of a savage trim), because she had lost some, and it had been looking a little unhealthy due to some of her medications.

Emily slayed the biggest dragon she will ever slay last night by going to see her sister. It was a long, hard trip up that aisle. She stopped about halfway up and got stuck, unable to move forward or backward or lift her head. I called my good friend Dr. Jim Powell, who talked me through what to do with her. He told me it was fine if she quit and tried again tomorrow.

Larry and I decided earlier that day after that Emily and Caroline needed to see Sarah. Emily needed to see her perhaps to stop the nightmares. She has been talking to Sarah in her sleep. When I came back into the sanctuary from my phone call, I told Larry what I had decided, and he whispered that she had her head up. And she did. She was looking ahead, but not moving yet. Trenton Anderson was being the good big brother that he has been forever and was holding her. Aunt Karmen and Baylee were right there. Larry was amazed at how articulate Baylee was with Emily. Kisen and Raul were waiting at the front. Several people who had come in were waited in the lobby while Emily did this big thing privately. We asked her if she wanted to go look at the signature board, and she said yes.

When we got to the front of the chapel, she pulled toward Sarah and went there instead. She cried for a bit and then started advocating for her sister. She said that the undershirts were not on in the correct order, and she wanted that fixed. She wanted her bangs fixed, because they were not right, and she wanted either her makeup fixed or the light above her changed out, because the makeup looked too orange. I had thought that there was something not quite right about the makeup, but I couldn't place it. Then I realized it was the orange.

Emily had brought a set of dog tags that she had made for her and Sarah three years ago; she had found it in Sarah's room yesterday. She put them in with her. Then after making sure that they were going to fix the things that were not right, she said, "I am ready to go home." She was brave and strong and observant.

Today Mom is coming over, and we are going to try to get her in the shower. Caroline is going to try to go see Sarah today. She is just being Caroline, the little mother hen, like she always has been. "Mom, have you eaten?" "Mom, have you slept?" It seems that I am sleeping every other night and eating every other day.

Sometimes I think that I am sleepy or hungry, and when it hits me, I have got to sleep right then or have to have food right then. Cathy Peetom brought chicken noodles that were perfect and very farmer wife-ish. Someone named Desiree brought a pasta meal, salad, bread, and desert that I ate some of last night. The dessert was still warm.

Several people have brought things right out of the over that are still warm. I don't know what it is about food being warm that strikes me as love, love, love.

Blake will be reading a letter from his dad. Yesterday he got Emily out of the house and took her for Chinese. His fortune cookie said something about having a letter that someone was waiting for.

I just don't know . . .

I am amazed at the outpouring of love from across the country that has come to us. Our friends from Facebook, AJ's, the school systems, our old college friends has been . . . we just have no words. Sarah even received a plant from the Canton football team.

Her school picture just arrived. Bluncks was able to fast-forward an eight-by-ten to us. It is perfect. Janice brought it over to me after it arrived at the school. Larry and I just so happened to drop by the funeral home to see her when Janice was delivering it. It was breathtaking how beautiful it is. It is perfect. We both cried over it.

A parent of one of my students dropped by this morning with her baby, and he was *hilarious*. He doesn't hug; he just leans in and closes his eyes. So cute. Her relative lives across my alley and heard me screaming Sarah's name in the backyard that night, but didn't know that I was Cantrell's teacher. That night seems like a million years ago.

We are leaving in a few minutes for a candlelight vigil for Sarah in Lamont and Blackwell. We grow good kids around here.

I did have a huge disappointment today. A friend who has been calling and texting me to tell me she is praying for me has been talking ugly about my Sarah. I want everyone to know that anytime there is a fatal accident, blood is drawn from those involved. Both Sarah and Michael tested negative for alcohol. I have been very straightforward from the beginning of this situation, and I would have been straightforward about that as well. But neither my child nor her friend were drunk. When you judge other people, you do not define who they are; you define who you are.

Emily went to see the car. They wouldn't let her in to see it, and she was *pissed*. She has been mad all evening, and that is better than her being on the couch with her head under the covers. She did see it from a distance, and she went to the scene.

The product safety investigator was here today. He has been to the scene and the car to look at the tire. I can't remember the word he said, but the tread had completely separated from the tire, and the tire was still inflated. There is a name for this. He said a NASCAR driver couldn't have driven out of it. It was not a retreaded tire or an old tire. It was a bad tire. Manufacture defect, he said.

Peace and grace be yours in abundance.

September 27

The vigils were perfect. I am just so exhausted tonight. Emily has already fallen asleep here beside me in bed. She is letting us touch her now. I just can't tell you what a relief that is.

Sarah's name was on the bank marquee in Lamont, and the town made Emily and me prayer quilts with every knot tied by another person who had prayed over it. What a powerful blessing. Larry was very moved today when Coach Hutchinson came and brought us her cross country jersey signed by all the team.

We stood with three of my little friends, one of whom was pretty sure that the candle was for his birthday (which isn't until summer); one wanted to know when Monday is, because that is when I am coming back. She is fairly certain that Mrs. Schuermann and Mrs. Black are trying to kill them all. They made them walk *in the street*, for pity's sake (they went on a nature walk). I asked the three friends if Mrs. Shuermann and Mrs. Black were doing a good job and they said, "No," and solemnly and bravely shook their heads. This is hilarious to me for some reason.

Their little world is upside down. I asked one little friend if he got to see Emily when we came to the school (he really digs Emily), and he said, "Yeah, when you and that boy came to our room." That boy is Larry. I said, "Oh, you mean Mr. Desbien. He is the papa at our house." "No, my papa is over there."

Then at the Blackwell candle vigil, we had an opportunity to laugh at what a *horrible* driver Sarah was. It takes a special kind of monkey to bend two rims in three places, put bulges on two tires, and have skid marks under the fender of a *four-wheel-drive* vehicle in a simple *curb check.*

We talked to Don (Larry's brother), who saw the purple sunset the other night.

It is good to hear memories of Sarah.

We have found out about an article about Sarah that was on the sports page of the Enid newspaper.

What is really weird to me is seeing her name on the marquee and in the paper and on the board at the funeral home. Something about seeing her name and realizing it is *my* Sarah they are talking about breaks my heart all over again. It all comes back in a rush of emotion.

We had so much to do today that I didn't get to see my mom much today. I am missing her. I hope she was as loved and supported today as we were.

Peace and grace be yours in abundance.

September 28

I am just so cold.

Emily woke up a couple of hours ago and said that it was going to be weird not waking up to Sarah talking in her sleep. The funny thing is, Sarah and I used to find some of the things Emily said in her sleep hilarious. We would even try to talk to her to keep it going. We would ask her questions very quietly. But she is right; we will miss her talking in her sleep, making us laugh even in the middle of the night.

As we stumble through parts of these days, we remember little things that she did at various times in the day, like sitting in the living room cross-legged, straightening her hair and laying her straightener on a pot holder. Listening to her music in her rocking chair with one headphone out so she could always hear . . . She was great.

I will miss her in the mornings. I think back to some hellacious mornings around here—all three of my girls after they started caring about their hair. It was not a pretty thing in my bathroom in the morning. Not a lot of mirror space or counter space. We had two other bathrooms, but the other bathrooms didn't offer that great opportunity to kick off the day with an elbowing, screaming match.

We always shared things, ate off each other's plates, slept together sometimes, and drank from the same glass. But one thing that I never wanted to share with my child is my plot at the cemetery. I had purchased a plot by my dad a while ago for myself. Today that is where Sarah will be buried.

It is still just so far away from anything I can fathom. She did this big thing without me to walk her through it.

Building relationships. Creating experiences. Service to others.

Peace and grace by yours in abundance.

September 29

Sarah and Emily's dad came. We all wondered if he would. Their brother came in and stood beside me, and as I walked toward the door, Mom told me that their dad was "out there." Mom handled herself beautifully, because I had asked her to. I lay here kind of snickering now, because she wanted to scratch his eyeballs out.

Larry had a really rough day, but he was so loving. Last night after everything was done, Larry and I both were so tired, but the family had gone out to our business to turn on the karaoke system and listen to our cousin sing. They asked Larry and me to come, but we initially said no. Caroline and Blake said they would stay with Emily (because I didn't want her left alone), and we went out. We stood outside the door for just a moment, holding each other before we went in.

I really didn't think I was going to be able to go in to the service. As we started down the aisle, I heard Larry whisper, "Wow." There were over a thousand people at her service, and they were in purple.

When we got down front and there was her casket, I just couldn't stop shaking and panicking. When our friend Fred started singing, I just closed my eyes. As he sang, I felt more and more calm. I thought he did a beautiful job.

The slide show didn't work, but we still played the music. It was perfect.

Blake read a letter from his dad. I don't know where he found the words, but they were perfect. He talked about a football incident in the letter, and we all laughed. One time Mom and the girls and I had all gone to Copperas Cove before he deployed. We were all in a little park with ducks and picnic facilities. He was standing on one side of the ravine, and Ronnie yelled, "Hey, son, see if you can catch this one." So we naturally all turn to look. (Some of the experiences that are funniest for us and most painful for Ronnie have begun with the words "Hey, son." This would include the skateboard in Toys R Us that ended, I believe, with a concussion, and the skateboard on the driveway that ended with broken wrists.) So Ronnie had yelled, and everyone had turned. He ran through with his kick like he was kicking a kickoff. Somehow or another his back leg kicked his front leg, and his whole body lifted up in the air and turned, and he came down in a dirt belly buster. All the dust and fall leaves kind of went "poof" around him. It was one of those times when we literally fell on the ground laughing and couldn't even help him up. When we got home, he was trying to dig his Copenhagen out of his front pocket; it had broken and was smashed flat. Many hours later, Karmen and I would dissolve into a fit of hysteria, and he would just sit there very droll.

He mentioned our dad giving people nicknames, and Dad always did. Tyler was Cowboy. Kelsey was Toothless. Tisha was Whistle Britches. Tisha would tell him, "My name is *not* Whittle Brittes!"

I was struck by how articulate and poised the kids who spoke were.

One of the songs that we played was "No More Night" by David Phelps. Larry chose that. In fact, all the songs were chosen by someone. I chose "I Can Only Imagine." Mom chose the song that Fred sang, "I Believe." Emily, Mitch, and Caroline chose "If I Die Young." Sarah chose "Sarah Smiles," which was her favorite song. She also chose "Imagine." That song really spoke to her. Ronnie chose "One Sweet Day.' As Shelly was leaving the house the night Sarah died, the song "Brown Eyed Girl" came on the radio. She called me back just devastated. It was the perfect song for us to leave our family and friends with. Caroline, Emily, Larry, and I planned the music before the service.

Toward the end of the service, Mr. Zachery came over to me and asked if we want them to sing the school song instead of "Eagle Pride." I told him that I had to have "Eagle Pride.*"* So the DCLA kids got up and did it. It was hilarious and perfect. Sarah had seen it the first time on Friday, and she loved it. You can imagine her long legs and fluid body movements as she did it. Claws out, wings up, feet apart, knees together, tail out, head a-bobbin', walking around. Eagle Pride! Eagle Pride! WHOOP! WHOOP! Eagle Pride! Eagle Pride! WHOOP! WHOOP! Then, as they were all hugging us, they broke into an impromptu singing of the school song. It was perfect.

My house has been filled with kids with big feet and broken hearts and empty stomachs. It is now time for them to move forward and away from the grief and shock.

There is a great book that I read to children when we have a loss in my classroom (typically it has been when a pet or grandparent has died). It is called *The Ten Good Things about Barney*. A boy's cat dies, and he is supposed to make a list of ten good things about his cat. He can only think of nine, until he asks his dad what will happen to Barney when he is buried. His dad tells him that Barney will help the flowered grow. So the tenth good thing is helping flowers grow, and that is a pretty good job for a cat. I found several of Sarah's lists, but I just can't make my own about her right now. I may read this to my class, as they are reeling too. They all loved Sarah.

When talking to young children (who often have fear as one of their primary emotions when dealing with death), there are several things they need to know. (1) All living things die. If it is alive, whether it be grass, an animal, or a person it will die. (2) All functions stop when someone dies. They are not asleep. They are not breathing or hurting or swallowing. (3) Death is permanent. People say that violence in video games is a problem, and I agree with that. But for me the more critical issue is that there is no permanence in video-game death; restart your game, and there they are.

Wish I had me a reset button.

Children also need to know that while everyone dies (they make the connection that that means them too), no one ever dies unless they are too sick, too hurt, or too old to get better.

I will be posting the video that was supposed to play. The picture of her with the two kids was a Christmas gift-giving thing that we did. The piece of her dancing had just been taken by her sister about two weeks ago on her cell phone. That is her shuffling and wearing her Grinch slippers.

Emily is furious because she cannot go to school today, but I can't go yet. And I don't want her there by herself, and I can't have her on the highway. Her birthday is next Wednesday.

Peace and grace be yours in abundance.

September 29

Cats really don't care what you are going through. If you don't clean their kitty litter box, they are going to defecate in the shower—twice.

I can't get the video to load, but Caroline is going to try. I am usually very technologically savvy, and I can do a lot of things, but I just can't do it. It is my plan that it go up today, and it is great.

Several friends were here when it arrived, and we all sat around the computer screen watching it in the dark. Faces glowing with smiles and the light from the computer monitor. Laughing at her silly shuffle in the Grinch slippers.

We went to the doctor for my cold and did shopping therapy for Emily. She bought a beta and named him Joe. She always called Sarah Joe, and it ticked her off.

Emily: Way to go, Joe.

Sarah: Stop calling me Joe!

Emily: Okay, Joseph. [Sarah punches Emily.] OUCH!

It was pretty hard venturing out with Caroline and Emily. I have been out in the last couple of days, but not with just my crew. The girls and I went everywhere together. It was a very quiet drive; we were all thinking the same thing. When we got to Newkirk, Robert was doing road work with the crew as one of the little road guys who hold the slow sign, so we had to yell some smack at him about being *slow*.

We talked to Dr. Veal to get something for Emily to relieve her headache. This doctor, who had helped us work through Sarah's depression through therapists and medication, said that when she saw Sarah last week for her cross country physical, she had never been happier. She sat with us for about thirty minutes and cried. That is the mark of a true physician: one who heals more than your physical ailments. Got a shot in the hind end for my sinus infection today. My hip aches. There's something comforting about that pain.

There are a few things that have tasted really good. Today when we went to Walmart, and Caroline got some beef jerky, and that was really good.

I have decided that the reason I am so quick in transitions from awake to sleep and not hungry to starving is because I have become very primitive in function. All my energy is going to my head and heart, and taking care of the critical need there, so the rest of my body is having to function on auto pilot.

Got an aquarium for my classroom and some Duplo blocks; got a coloring book and new crayons for each of my students. Got some thank-you notes.

The investigator has called twice today to discuss the tire. I haven't answered; I can't talk about that today. Missed my brother's call twice. In the mail today came the papers from my health and life insurance for the girls and me. I always buy that for us when working at a school. It's ironic that the papers arrived today.

Very tired.

Peace and grace be yours in abundance.

September 29

Tomorrow list:

1. Take Emily to school. I hope she makes out okay. She will be dropping off coloring books and crayons for each student in my class. I will not be going in. I don't want us to be a distraction.
2. Buy some shampoo.
3. Do laundry

4. Put Emily on the bus to Covey for her football managing duties, I guess.
5. Follow five feet behind bus in my car.

September 30

Cannot remember my logon to check my school e-mail. Hmmm.

Went out on Highway 60 to look at the crane at about ten tonight. It is a sight to behold.

Emily has been asleep for most of the evening. I think she finally has some relief from the head pain and sleeplessness.

That is all.

Peace and grace be yours in abundance.

September 30

I want to address the rumors about Michael and Dereck dying. Michael has been to our house every day. Yesterday I slept on the couch with a house full of people. When I woke, there was his mom, sitting vigil over me. I was on Larry's computer one day, and there was Michael, sitting quietly. No words, just company. He is struggling. Please, please, please pray for him. If you notice him start to slide, please tell his mama.

When I prayed for my babies, I always prayed for health, wealth, peace, and safety. Health so that they were never infirm. Wealth so that they never knew cold or hunger. Peace so that their souls could be at rest and playful. Safety so that they never know pain.

When I sleep now, I sleep hard. No dreaming. I am awake, and then I am asleep, which is very unusual for me. Typically, I linger over sleep with drowsiness, thinking, and when I get up in the morning, it is with guns blazing. Now that is reversed; I go to sleep very quickly and get up with the thinking. I wake up saying her name. Could I be dreaming about her and not realizing it? Once I wake up, that is it—no sleepiness. Seems like my body is taking just what it needs to function.

When I woke up this morning, that prayer was on my mind. Health, wealth, peace, and safety. In the end, I only provided the one that didn't really matter.

You know it is funny the things that have occurred to me. Twenty-two years ago this month, my dad was buried on a Wednesday and on Friday of that week, my brother boarded a bus for the football game that took him right by Dad's accident scene. Today, following her sister being buried on a Wednesday, Emily will board a bus for the football game that will take her right by the accident scene. It is all I can do not to drive to Lamont to follow the bus. But Larry and I will leave from here and go directly to Langston.

Emily did go to school this morning. She said it was very hard to get up with the house so quiet, because Sarah always got up first—not a lot of fighting for counter space. Seems weird that it was just a week ago that I had all these teenagers getting ready for Spirit Day in my classroom.

Emily and I stopped for Starbucks for coffee this morning. Trying to find some new rituals. We went to Turtles, and she bought pastries for the staff.

When we got to school, they were happy to see her. Seems as though there may have been some wagering going on as to how long I could stay away from my babies. I wasn't going to let them see me, so when they went to breakfast, I sneaked into the room and laid out their coloring books, crayons, and some donut holes. I remember back to the beginning of the year; on Thursdays I would tell them, "One more day of school and two days home with Mom." That always seemed to soothe them when the week was getting long. Today one of my little friends said, "Only two days at home and then you come back, Teacher." One little friend said that she had done a really good job at nap time. (She cries sometimes at nap time, and

I have heard that she is struggling most of the day. She has had a setback.)

Music sounds really good right now.

Fridge is cleaned out and organized, laundry going, dishes done.

Last night the doorbell rang at 10:15, which scared me to death. I asked the kid in the living room who was at the door, and he didn't recognize her. I asked if it was a law enforcement officer.

Larry took the Durango to get it fixed from Sarah's curb check that tore up the rims and tires. Instead of having the tires repaired, he replaced all four and the spare.

I am trying to show a lot of grace and dignity, but can I just tell you how much I hate ambulance chasers that misrepresent themselves.

Larry and I are going to the game.

Had a list of twelve things to get done today. Completed one and a half.

September 30

Tonight before the game, after the little huddle, Coach told them, "Let's go out and have a fancy game." The Coyle announcer had a moment of silence for my child and the father-in-law of Coach. After every touchdown, Connor's mom, Barbara, held up a sign that said, "Sarah Smiles." After the Eagles won and the game was called at halftime due to the mercy rule, the team huddled and then coach came running across the field and climbed up the railing to where Larry and I were standing with the crowd, waiting for the kids. He slipped a purple wristband on my sleeve that was similar to what the whole team had worn. He hugged me and said, "It was a great night." Then the team came to the sideline and took off their cleats, stepped onto the track, and sang the school song. After they sang, every one of those boys climbed the railing to hug me and tell me, "Love you, Mrs. Desbien." All I could say was, "Good boys. What good boys." My heart is broken, but it is full.

October 1, 2011

It doesn't bother me to see young people. It bothers me to see old women and wonder why Sarah didn't get to be an old woman.

I want to sleep all the time. I have always been a light sleeper, but now there is this deep, deep hole where I go to sleep. The phone doesn't even rouse me. Very unusual—no dreams, no rest, just sleep.

I do not want to see anyone today. I am sorry for them, but these people still have their children. They need to take them home and heal them there. Some people that barely knew her and that I had lost touch with are dropping by the house. I am just tired of other moms sniffling and crying at my house. Go cry at your own house with your kids that are alive.

Mom is handling all legal matters. I can't do it.

Sarah had $98.43 in her savings account. Her funeral cost over fourteen thousand dollars.

I still do mom stuff like take an armful of laundry up as I go, wipe a counter off as I walk by.

How is this part of my life story? How is this part of the tapestry of my life?

I am getting a pumpkin tomorrow.

I woke up thinking about her feet.

Emily is just so angry.

For the past two years, Emily's birthday has been overshadowed because of Sarah—a hospital stay, a grounding. Recently Sarah had told Emily teasingly, "Wait until you see what I do this year."

I found her two-layered shirts that she wore for picture day. She had peeled them off and thrown them in the laundry basket still together. I can't separate them to wash them in the appropriate loads. So I hid them.

Last night on the way to the game, I put a CD in and sang as loud as I could.

Today in the mail: her bank savings account statement and the accident claim form from the insurance company.

Emily is thumping around in her room. I think she is cleaning it.

The last load of laundry is in the dryer.

I did it.

October 2

Went to flea market and then Lowes to look for part of Emily's birthday. Now home. Downloaded *Death of a Salesman* onto Netflix for the girls to watch. I never got the chance to show it to her.

Someone signed me up for a grieving mother's Facebook site, and it said, "Welcome to Grieving Mothers" to me. Are you kidding? Really?

October 3

The dreams have started.

One of my little friends said today, "Teacher, I don't like that . . . what happened to Sarah."

As we were walking up the hall, one friend stopped very suddenly, sucked in her breath, and said, "Oh! I just remembered about Sarah!"

Another friend: "Don't you ever say that again. It will make Teacher cry!"

I don't know, sometimes I just stop and suck in my breath and remember about her.

Returned to school today. Emotional on the way over. Very busy day. Set up the aquarium. Cannot tend to the kids, because all I can think about is Sarah. Emily has good and bad times. I need to see more of Caroline.

I think I know how the accident happened. It occurred to me last night that she was not buckled.

I am exhausted. I am weary of missing her already. It has been one week. I now don't mark time looking forward to anything, I mark time as moments endured.

Words have always been a soother for me. I have no words. I do not want to speak. I want to sit mute and observe nothing.

As bad as it is, I have no regrets. As parents, we can always do better. I could have listened to every little story; I could have checked on her more in the night; I could have not let her go that night. But by in large, I have no major regrets.

She and Emily and Caroline (like all children) were entitled to the best I had, and I think I gave it to them. But I did not keep her free from harm. I didn't make decisions for her. She had told me once that she was weak, and I told her that I was taking over decision making. I had recently let her begin making decisions again, and I knew that she was not being forthcoming.

"Ma'am, I need you to talk to me." That was what the officer said.

Just texted the girls to make sure they were buckled up. They and Mitch went to get ice cream. Mitch sent me a picture of the girls buckled up. Some random person called me to tell me that she is praying for me and to remind me that she knows how I feel—she had lost her husband in a car accident. No, you don't know how I feel. You did not lose a human being who had passed through you, who you were responsible for keeping alive until she was eighteen. You didn't fail to protect your child.

How is this a part of my life story? It is a nightmare.

October 4

I cannot think about her. It hurts too much. When she pops into my mind, I push it aside. If I think about her, I will go crazy. Some people say that I am strong, but I am avoiding. I am a fraud.

I should have been a better mother to her. I should have done more to save her. She deserved better. I am no better than her father.

I am marking the days off without Sarah. I am almost two weeks without her. Feels like an accomplishment, but now what?

I didn't cry today. I have been pretty angry. I cannot deal with the insurance and all that stuff. Cannot. Will not.

Today, toward the end of the day, I was staring off into space and one of the little friends asked, "What's wrong, Teacher?" I said, "Just thinking." She came up to me and wrapped her little arms around me and patted my back and whisper sang, "Twinkle, Twinkle, Little Star" into my ear. While she was doing it, another little boy came and kissed me on the lips and rubbed my arms. They don't have words, but there is such truth to their actions. Such sweet little ones . . .

I woke up at midnight remembering the softball to the face. The second I got to the mound, she said, "It hurts, Mom. It hurts so bad." I ran to the car with her, not grabbing my purse or any of my stuff. Shelly Braden was with me and brought it all. I threw her in the car, and we raced from Kids, Inc., to the ER in eleven minutes. They were messing with paperwork, and she quietly knelt down and started vomiting. Always like her to never want to be a bother. She was so sweaty and pale and clammy. Then they took her for her CT scan, and she just took it all in.

One morning we had a wreck on the way to school, and she just took all that in as well. Never cried, just observed.

I didn't save her from herself . . .

Little friend while coloring: Sarah can see us.

Another little friend: Yep, she is in the stars.

Yet another little friend: Well, probably not the stars, but for sure in heaven.

Other little friend: Yep, with Jesus.

Last little friend: Yep.

"Ma'am. I need you to talk to me. Ma'am, I need you to talk to me." He said that twice as he stepped toward me with his hand outstretched. When I threw my phone, it broke a plate on my wall that said "Family."

October 5

Fifteen years ago this morning, I was awakened a little before 2:30 with my first contraction. Two hours and twenty-nine minutes later, Emily Jane arrived. As I was being wheeled out of the delivery room holding her, her granny and two big sisters were there to give her first dose of love. I love you, Emily. I love the sister, daughter, and person you are. When I grow up, I want to be more like you.

Mom met with the investigator and the highway patrolman today. I do not want to go to school tomorrow. I just want to sleep in my recliner all day and forever. I miss my girl so much.

If he had gotten off the brakes, he could have driven out of it.

The highway patrol was there within five minutes.

She was still breathing when she reached the hospital.

There was never any hope.

October 6

Not today.

I am remembering quite a bit about that night. Last night was particularly difficult, as a lot of stuff came back. I do not remember the faces of the officers that came that night. All I remember are the uniforms. One of them gave Larry his card. I don't even know their names.

There was this one Mother's Day that Sarah had been working and saved up all her money. She had made reservations for the two of us at Zino's. When we got there, she laid her little crayon box on the table. When the menus came and we picked out our entrees, she got her money out of the crayon box and carefully counted it. After she figured what the total including tip would be, she told me that we could afford an appetizer. When the waitress brought the bill, Sarah told her, "I'll take that," and she paid. Sweetest thing . . .

DCLA and Sarah were on the *Channel 9 News*. I hope they are back on at ten. I missed it. Thankfully, my friend Barbara Kirby is making me a copy of it—saving me from my crying, stomping fit. She was also responsible for circling the DCLA wagons the night

Sarah died and getting Emily home from the dance. Once again, she comes to my rescue. We are so blessed that God placed us where He did at this time in our lives.

I think I have gotten a second wind today. Needed to regroup. Remembering some troubling things about that night and some memories of her that make my heart ache. I slept and thought and cried quite a bit today. I am amazed at how fragile I am.

I read one time about what you become when the water gets hot. Are you a carrot that gets soft? Are you an egg that gets hard, or are you a tea bag that infuses everything around you and spreads who you are with richness and warmth? I want to be a tea bag, but I am sure feeling like the carrot. Pretty limp and flimsy.

I never miss school, and I love, love, love my kids. They keep me busy and my mind off of it. I just knew I was not going to be able to hold it together today. I may not be able to do a full week for a while. I may have rushed going back. But perhaps if I can give my little friends a heads-up, it won't be so traumatic for them when I am gone. I think if I need to take a breather, I will text the mommies.

I truly believe that attitude is a choice, and I have always tried to choose to be positive. But let me tell you, I am struggling.

October 7

Focusing on others, and I have a few surprises planned for tomorrow. I also have a few projects planned. Trying to make a rocket pack for the dress-up center out of two pop bottles. How cool is that?

I am letting Emily ride the football bus to Southwest Covenant and back home. Larry and I will not be going to the game, and I will be a wreck the entire time she is gone. But my head knows that if I don't let her do some things, she will be worse off in the long run. So, I have to loosen the grip I have on her.

One thing that I have come to realize is that grief is hard enough without regrets. Caroline, Emily, and I have talked a lot about the fact that we have no regrets. We were always very vocal and passionate about life, and we fought and made up and loved loudly and laughed at and with each other, and what did we not let happen is words go unspoken, feelings go unexpressed, moments go unexperienced.

A little friend brought me cookies today because "you can't get feeling better, Teacher."

Took bagels and spread by to the teachers at Lincoln.

The evening is the time of day that I miss her most. Her knocking around the house, just out of the shower, hair up in a towel in a long T-shirt, munching on an apple, one headphone in, plopping down on the couch, asking what she should wear tomorrow, or saying, "Hey, Mom. I got a question."

October 8

Have Emily home safe and sound from the treacherous bus ride. Caroline and Mitch are tucked in at their house. Just talked to Mom. Larry and I had a nice visit to and from Lamont to get our girl. Good as it can be.

It felt really good to laugh hard twice in the last twenty-four hours:

1. Concerning the toll booth and the bus, and my daughter having to contribute $1.50—that is hilarious. Mom has called twice today, laughing about that.
2. Something about Pop-Tarts—about dropped a lung. It was so funny.

Mom and I had a good talk tonight, rehashing and reassuring each other. There will always be guilt and what-ifs.

I don't know what to say when people ask me how many children I have.

We have some more service projects that we are working on, concerning the team, the school, and society at large.

But for tonight, I am crocheting Emily a red, white, and blue hat (the kind with long braids). I had made her and Sarah both a blue and purple variegated hat before school started (those are their favorite colors). They loved them so much that they wore them in the summer. Larry said that they were the ugliest hats he had ever seen. He has no style whatsoever.

Tomorrow I am repotting a plant, working on thank-you notes, cleaning house, and hopefully working on some rocket packs for my recess time.

Peace and grace be yours in abundance.

October 8

OMG! Larry is so unhip! He saw a picture of Sarah with ♥ on it. He said, "What is less than three?" I just paused for a moment, not understanding what he meant. Then I saw it on the picture. <3 He is such a mathematician.

October 9

Can't do it today. Been a really rough night, just up and down, thinking about her and missing her and being in shock that she is gone. People look at me and whisper.

I think that I have lost some friends. I think that they think I am contagious.

Lying on the couch with Emily, watching *American Dad*.

She is everywhere I look. I was thinking of us playing Apples to Apples, and she just absolutely killed us at it. She was unbeatable. Every time she won a hand, she yelled, "Booyah!"

I was remembering how she did my frog bulletin board and my Peanuts bulletin board. She said that my kids had better appreciate it, because it was freaking hard to get it up. She would pound on the stapler yelling, "Take that, Snoopy!"

Her hair was so thick and luxurious. It had so much body; it was very different than mine. It was like Lisa's. She wasn't the least bit tender headed. I will miss touching her hair.

She worked so hard at yard work and house work. Helping people move, mow, paint, etc. She never minded getting sweaty and hot. She had helped me move my classroom I don't know how many times.

I should have done more to save her from herself. Gotten her more counseling, been stricter, tougher. Called her bluff more often.

October 10

Tonight I found her baby book with her little footprints in it.

When she was first born and they took her away, she was gone for four hours. I thought those were the longest four hours of my life—until now.

My mom painted her fingernails on the day we came home from the hospital.

She got two baby teeth on the same day.

October 11

Well, today was the best day that I have had so far. A lot of work and assessments at school that kept me very busy, plus we painted today. Any day with paint or glitter is a great day.

Emily and I had some good teenager/mom chat time today. It was good to talk about some nonsense teenage stuff instead of everything that has been going on. I think it was good for her to just go get a coke and talk about Emily.

Caroline and Mitch are on their way over with Sonic drinks, and Larry is home. Pillsbury (one of Sarah's *great* friends is over visiting). If Mom were here, it would be perfect—but Emily and I went to see her earlier.

It goes without saying that Sarah is on my mind constantly and aching in my heart.

October 12

Jeez, nighttime is rough. Well, looks like I will not be sleeping in my bed tonight, even though Emily is asleep already. I think it could be a restless night.

October 13

There is something horribly nightmarish about seeing the name that I fretted about choosing and hoped would be as special as my baby, typed so businesslike on a death certificate. It arrived today.

This evening, we heard some information concerning Sarah's injuries that we had not heard before, and it was different from what we heard in the first few days. It is heartbreaking. It has been a very troubling evening and in fact has been a setback, I think. Spent a lot of time pacing and heart-aching tonight.

Three and a half more days of school, then we are going away for a few days.

We also started designing her headstone. I don't know what the final product will be, but I hope it will have the word *fancy* on it.

Got a very special gift in the mail from my brother today from Afghanistan. It is a flag that flew on his helicopter. It flew on September 6, which was the twenty-second anniversary of our dad's accident. The mission that this flag went on lasted 4.8 hours. Dad's birthday was 4/8/48. The flag came with an autographed picture with the entire crew.

Emily and I are hitting Starbucks in the morning for our new Friday ritual. That will be a good pick-me-up for us. Pumpkin Spice Latte or Caramel Apple Spice. Hmmm, I could just get a black coffee with nothing fattening or creamy. Pshaw! As if I could do that!

October 14

Going to watch the Eagles do their thing. First home game since that night. But it is a beautiful night, I have a handsome date, and I feel a halftime mercy rule coming on.

I have spent a lot of time thinking about why she was taken and not someone else. Why was it *my Sarah*? And I think that her work here was done. We still have work to do. I still have work to do. I don't know what that is for any of us. But the only sense I can make out of it is that we still are on our mission. The best thing I can do to maintain my sanity and to honor Sarah is to discover what that mission is and go to it. And we will see her again in heaven and in our dreams and in our memories and in the wind, and when we look into our hearts. She is everywhere.

Emily's hands look like Sarah's when she drives. The way she wraps her fingers around the steering wheel looks the same.

October 15

When we used to go to Hunan's, she would eat a ton of cocktail shrimp and rice with lots of red sauce. She could eat like half a watermelon by herself. She and I made this fantastic pinwheel meatloaf with ham and Swiss cheese rolled in the middle like a jellyroll. If she wanted to cook something special for someone, she cooked a meatloaf. She loved fruit and baked potatoes. At Perkins, she always ordered the turkey and dressing dish.

To address rumors that are going around about our family:

1. Sarah was not drunk or high the night she died. There was blood drawn on both her and Michael that night and possibly the other passenger, but I do not know.
2. Michael was not her boyfriend; he was just a friend.
3. Emily is not an atheist. But it is hard for her to discuss her relationship with God, angels, and heaven when there is a huge hole where her heart used to be.
4. Emily is not medicated out of her gourd. She is on headache medication and occasionally something to help her sleep. That is all.
5. To our knowledge Sarah was not pregnant. She had been to the doctor the week before for a full physical and had been to the doctor countless times in the last few months due to her poor health. Nothing was revealed in these doctor's appointments or extensive testing.
6. Emily is not continuously crying and asking for her sister. She is trying to get through the days like we all are. She is just having a rougher time, because people are texting her stupid stuff.
7. Caroline is not pregnant. She has had an intestinal bug and has been throwing up for a week.
8. We do not know if Sarah had on a seatbelt. We have been told both things. We do not have the accident report. It should come anytime now. Mom set down with the highway patrolman who worked the accident, and he told her that if she had been seat belted behind the driver, we would not have been able to have an open casket. Also Mom was told the back seat was unsurvivable. This was probably one of the few situations that a seatbelt would not have made a difference and could have made it worse.
9. We are strong, but some days we are just really good actresses. Part of the reason we have been able to be so strong is because we were blessed to have the miracle that was Sarah for sixteen years. We loved hard, fought hard, played hard, worked hard. At the end of the day, there was nothing left unsaid, nothing left undone. We have no regrets

and a lot of memories. We also have been able to be strong because we have the love and support and prayers of good and decent people.

There is this teenager who will not quit texting Emily and telling her that I said Sarah was pregnant and it showed up in the autopsy. Supposedly I told her mom at our business.

1. I do not go to our business since Sarah died, except to drop off supplies.
2. I do not talk to people I don't know about Sarah, and I certainly wouldn't have talked to someone I don't know about something as intimate as that.
3. I don't know this girl's mom.
4. There was no autopsy. It was not an unattended death. After the accident, blood was drawn for the drug and alcohol test. Although she lived a few minutes, there was never any hope that she would survive. We were asked to donate tissue but not organs.
5. After Emily told her that I don't know this mom, she then said that she heard the rumor from another person that comes into our business—a person that is only an acquaintance of mine that I have not seen in months.
6. Sarah was under a doctor's constant supervision due to the fact that she had chronic respiratory and intestinal health issues that she had battled all her life. She had extensive frequent tests and blood work done. A pregnancy never showed up in any of these tests.
7. We are not perfect, and neither was Sarah. We would have not cared if Sarah had been pregnant. We would have loved any baby that came into our lives in any way it came. But according to all information that we have, there was no pregnancy.
8. We have been very open and honest about everything we know. We would not hide something as miraculous as a baby.

How do I get this person to leave my kid alone?

Missing in America was a movie that Sarah had recently watched. She watched several times and cried every time she watched it. She said that it caught her off guard and wasn't how it was supposed to end.

She named all her babies Jessica when she was little, but she always said if she ever had a daughter, she was going to name her Lyla or Lillian or Lillie.

We will not be wasting any more energy on power suckers. Our energy will be going to other things. We will be choosing to look away.

October 16

Cooked for the first time today since we lost Sarah. Had a fit when I couldn't find my favorite skillet. But after I calmed down and was able to think, I walked right to the cabinet it was in. It felt good to get back to that part of myself.

Emily has had another bad morning after the bully messing with her a little more. I think we have it taken care of. We have made it very clear that we will be going to the police if she doesn't leave us alone. We are choosing to be positive, but we are also choosing to be advocates for our peace.

October 17

I don't remember if I posted these stories about Sarah, but I was thinking about them tonight:

1. One time I woke up in the morning and couldn't find her. I frantically looked for her and finally found her, asleep under her bed. She had fallen out of bed, rolled under it, and fallen back asleep.
2. One time we fell asleep watching a movie. Somehow she fell off the couch, jumped up and said, "I'm okay." Got right

back on the couch and fell right back to sleep. Emily and I were rolling laughing at her.

October 18

Three troubling thoughts swimming around in my head. Can't even type them tonight . . . obituaries, a lost chance, punishment. I can sort out one thing at a time, and in the beginning, I thought pretty slowly. But now, as my head is clearer, things occur to me too quickly.

October 20

Eureka Springs—a place where no one knows us. No one knew Sarah, and still she is everywhere.

Not going in the haunted hotel. Don't care how much Emily and Larry try to shame me. I will be sitting in the car crocheting. Psychos!

Probably should not have gone into the Christmas Store.

Later: So I went into the Haunted Hotel. Took some skeptical picture. Ghost totally showed up in one. Probably a hoax. Scared the crap out of me.

October 21

Trying very hard not to overprotect and shelter Emily. She and Mitch are on their way to Lamont to pick up a friend, and I am literally nauseated with worry. I guess this is my new normal—being paranoid and weak.

October 23

I have always looked forward to birthdays, holidays, events—loved the planning, shopping, execution of gatherings, the schedule and the count down. That is how I marked time, with an eye to the future.

Now my life has become this quiet, sacred vigil of marking the days off since she left. I now mark time with an eye to the past—one day without her, one week, and now one month. It seems like an hour and a lifetime.

How is it possible?

We received a paper from our insurance company today. Her name is nowhere on it. She is Loss Claim Number _____ for loss occurring on September 23, 2011.

Mom and I talked tonight at length about Sarah and losing her. She had such an old soul. She was born with wisdom and depth that I will never have. Perhaps she had a head start because she was never going to reach adulthood.

I am struck by the difference in the loss of my dad when I was eighteen and the loss of my child at forty. When Dad died, I was panic stricken and felt very vulnerable, and there was this sharpness to the pain. It seemed very fleeting, the pain. Although I missed him dearly and do still mourn him, I was still me as I worked my way through it. The loss of Sarah has more of an achiness to the pain, very deep and lasting and has more of a "settling in" feel to it. It is almost as if I have become paralyzed or lost a limb. A very fundamental part of me is gone, and I will never function the same again. The other part that is very different is that I was not responsible for my dad. Regardless of how I try to justify my parenting ability with all the good things I did, I was responsible for that baby girl—and I did not fulfill my duty to her.

There is less laundry, fewer dishes, more leftovers, no apples, painful smiles (if at all).

There will be no relationships that she will need my advice for, no late-night calls that the baby is coming, no hearing her name called at graduation, no sitting on the front row of the church, watching her wed the one.

I posted a few days ago about three things that were bothering me that I couldn't talk about. I think I can address them now.

1. As you know, Emily has had a problem with a girl who has been going around saying that Sarah was pregnant and that I had told her mom that it showed up in the autopsy (which never occurred). I so wanted to be able to find out definitively if she was, so I could shut her up. After the drug and alcohol tests were run on Sarah's blood, the sample was destroyed. Although I had a very open relationship with her and believe that she would have come to me or one of her sisters or Granny had she been pregnant, we will never know for sure. So I will never be able to shut that kid up.
2. The Tuesday before she died, Sarah had curb checked in our Durango. Had we grounded her like we should have, she would not have been in that car.
3. Blackwell's obituary cost ten times what Ponca City's did.

I am just treading water, not sinking, not drowning, not being devoured by sharks, but not swimming forward.

Peace and grace by yours in abundance.

October 24

"Teacher, what is wrong with Emily?"

"She is just having a bad day."

"Probably because Sarah died-ed."

October 27

"I love you, Mom."

"Love you more."

"Love you most."

"Love you more than most."

October 29

Tonight, as Larry and I were driving home from Lowe's after dark, the girls called to say that they were going to the haunted house in Tonkawa. I told him I was going to go home, put on my pajamas, fix some hot apple cider, relax, and have control of the remote control. Then it hit me: that was my plan the night Sarah died. I had just sat down with a class of V8 that night when there was a knock at the door. Tonight I panicked and called Caroline and Emily and begged them to be careful. I hate the feeling of fear as much as I do the feeling of loneliness.

October 30

I am finding that there is still quite a bit of who I am left, and there are some new parts that I like, and some new parts I don't like. But a part of me is gone.

I never finished her chair that we picked out the fabric for.

I never purchased her a bed after Emily got hers.

I never got her a car.

I never told her about the Gofrillas.

It could be my excuse to quit. I intend to make it my reason to be more.

October 31

Visited Sarah's grave today. It was windy, and a tattered and torn flower had blown from another grave. It was purple, of course.

November 2

A little friend of mine has been gone for a few days. Yesterday Emily came into the classroom and he said, "Hey, where is Sarah?"

I said, "Do you remember? She died."

"How did she get died?"

"She was in a car wreck."

"When did that bad wreck happen?"

"Before you were gone. Remember, I told you I would be gone for five days."

"Yeah, I forgot about that bad thing."

Also, since my little friend assured me yesterday that a new pair of shoes always makes you happy, I got a new pair of shoes today. Turns out, new shoes do make me a little happy.

Got some new ornaments today for my new Santa theme tree. Felt much better to look at Christmas stuff with a theme in mind. I was very diligent in looking for particular ornaments and not thinking about the difference between Christmas last year and this year. We found some beautiful stuff. As we were leaving, Emily picked out an angel for our mantle; she has long brown hair and pinecones by her feet. Emily thought it was an "earthy" angel. We will leave it up year-round.

Today when Mom was being prepped for surgery, they used colored tape for her IV. Yep, it was purple. :)

Emily is asleep—first time in a long time that she has fallen asleep before midnight. Bless her heart.

There have been some conversations about the fact that I do not cry at school and seem unemotional about the death of my child. No, I am not on medication. What happens at school and what happens when I am alone with my family are two very different things. I cannot allow myself to become emotional when I have fourteen very important and impressionable young people to care for. I miss her terribly, but I cannot be a wreck at school and do the job that I have been entrusted to do.

November 4

Tonight I found a picture of when she was in first grade. She got her five-hundred-book award on the same day I got my master's degree. It was a picture of both of us. She had her glasses on in the picture, and I thought back to a day when she was in first grade and came running into the teacher's lounge where I was. She was crying because she had forgotten her glasses. I had been trying to teach her natural consequences and told her that she would have to just do without them that day. She came to me in need, and I told her no, I would not go get the glasses. While I did take her glasses to her that day, the fact that I didn't comfort her and tell her not to worry and instead was very stern bothers me tonight. I miss her little brown eyes so much.

November 5

I am so thankful that I got to be Sarah's mom. I miss her incredibly. I hate, hate, hate that she is gone and that I will never see her hold her children, graduate from high school, move into a dorm. I learned so much from her, probably more than I taught her. I am a better person for having known her. My life is brighter because her light shone upon it. The world is more beautiful because she was here

Received the hospital bill. In the mail at the same time were some insurance papers that contained the accident report and death certificate. The information that was in those three pieces of paper was a little different than what I thought. First, we were told that she was killed instantly. Then that she had lived about fifteen minutes. But in truth, the time that elapsed between the accident and her death was fifty minutes. Those people worked for almost an hour trying to save my child. Bless their hearts.

November 7

After a *rough*, tearful couple of days, Emily is doing better this evening. Thankfully, she was finally able to open up and talk, and she found some peace tonight. Bless her heart. A fellow teacher told me today that if we could just answer the question "Why?" for her, she would be fine. So true.

November 11

Reading *The Shack*. Ronnie wanted me to read it, and even had Karmie buy it for me. I have had it sitting on my table for six weeks. Started it tonight.

Some friends will go to lunch with you. Some friends will exchange recipes with you. Some friends will drive you home from girls' night. Those are great friends to have.

However, some friends will come to your house in the middle of the night. They will come at the crack of dawn. They will actually go with you to the funeral home and help you pick out a casket in which to bury your child. Those friends are more than friends. They are sisters. I am so thankful that God blessed me with my "soul sisters," some of whom arrived within thirty minutes of us learning that we had lost our Sarah.

Larry still gets emotional when he talks about that first thirty minutes before they arrived. He says, "Until you got here, I didn't know what to do. She was just lying in the backyard, screaming."

Shelly, Merle Ann, and LeaAnne got here so fast. They cried with me and lay with me.

Shelly went to the funeral home with us to help plan the funeral and pick out the casket. She took a week off work to be with me. Staci and my other Shelly also came in the middle of the night. Tina and Laura were here the next morning as soon as they heard, bringing food, paper goods, hugs, and again with the tears. Lori texted me and said that she needed to come hug me. My response to her was, "Hurry." As mothers, it must have been incredibly frightening for them to be here, but here they were.

I have never been as lifted up as I was in those first few hours and days. I have never felt more loved. Even in the face of my worst nightmare, I have never felt more blessed to be surrounded by strong, order-seeking, sense-making women. There are some things that I simply do not remember. I remember lying on the porch with Shelly holding me. I remember Staci crying on the couch beside me. I remember Laura setting food in front of me, rubbing my back, and telling me, "Sweetie, just one bite. You have to have just one bite."

Sometimes I will remember a kind act: someone wiping my face with a cold rag as I threw up at the end of our porch that night, someone sitting with me and quietly crying while I slept, a drink being sat down in front of me. I do not know who did these simple things; I just know they were done. Even now, my life is full of kindness and remembrance and hope. It is a very bittersweet and beautiful place in which I find myself. A place of conflicting emotions of sadness and love—both so strong that they are impossible to articulate.

All I can say is, for these women I am thankful.

This week I started wearing makeup for the first time since Sarah died. Just haven't felt like it mattered. Apparently it does. A little friend of mind said, "Teacher, your eyes are *beautiful*!"

November 12

New insurance cards came in the mail today without Sarah listed as a dependent, along with a new statement with the adjustment of not having Sarah listed. Will cost a few dollars less each month. Also got a standard letter from the life insurance company: received documentation, very sorry for your loss, if you are found to be beneficiary, claim will be processed, blah, blah, blah. I always knew there would come a day when Emily would be my only dependent listed. I just thought it would be when Sarah finished college.

November 18

Larry and I were up in Emily's room, hanging her TV. I was looking at a framed eight-by ten of Sarah that Emily has in her room. It was taken last Thanksgiving. She is smiling and has on a purple shirt. I was just staring into her eyes, loving her, missing her. Then there was a loud knock at the front door that startled me. I have come to not like the loud knocks after dark. It was the postman, with a check made out to Lorrene Desbien, beneficiary of Sarah Ray.

November 19

I have never heard a more moving and uplifting talk as was given by our school's leader tonight. I have just never been a part of anything as exciting as this season has been. The healing and distraction that came from following this football team has been life saving for our family. I will carry the passion and fervor that this team showed for the rest of my days. I will love these boys, this school, this town, always.

Mom got stopped for going eighty-five miles an hour today. No insurance (it was a loaner vehicle) and some other trivial violations. Guess who got off with a warning. It was the same highway patrolman who worked Sarah's accident. Mom is sure Sarah is laughing at her.

November 20

Well, today was one of those tough days. I went to bed missing her and I woke up missing her and I have missed her all day. It is like this deep muscle bruise that no one can see but smarts like crazy.

Caroline and I were pretty busy working on one Service to Others project for tonight and shopping for a Service to Others project that will be delivered to the DCLA Junior and Senior High School at about 12:30 on Tuesday. Having those types of things to plan and execute are pretty cool. I miss having Sarah to help with the cooking. She would sit in the kitchen and talk to me and help and sample and text in her shorts and tank top and, of course, no shoes. As I was going to the store, I flipped on the radio and of course "Brown Eyed Girl" was playing. She is everywhere.

Part of the issue today was the depositing of the insurance. With it being made out to Lorrene L. Desbien, beneficiary of Sarah Ray, that was how I had to endorse it. The teller guy looked at me with such sadness and empathy. Sucks.

November 24

It is almost more than I can bear today.

Thanksgiving Day.

Well, today was tough. I knew it would be, but I was caught off guard by how raw the emotion was. After Emily and I made the goodies we were taking, and as I was putting on my makeup, I could hear Caroline, Mitch, and Emily knocking around the house and loading the goodies in the car. It was then that the tears started. Don't know where they came from—no warning, very unexpected. I was just putting on my makeup and then weeping. No sound, no sobbing, just a steady flow of tears that continued off and on for a few hours. It was quite unsettling to be talking to Mom with tears running down my cheeks. Again, no crying in the sense of any noise or chest convulsions or inability to speak, just this comfortable release of emotion. It was much like the relief that comes from a sneeze in that it was a bodily function that eased an irritation.

I was pretty fortunate to be surrounded by friends today. We had opened our business for some of our regulars. They all knew Sarah as this spicy little wisp who would bounce into the bar for chips, pop, and a few bucks and then bounce right back out. They of course offered no judgment—just hugs and compliments for my cooking—and they all brought wonderful food. We listened to music, played pool, and watched football on one TV, sitcoms on the other. Then Emily and I came home and slept for a few hours in between more of those weird silent tears.

November 26

She was left handed and loved pumpkin pie and could eat half a watermelon by her little self and made the most delicious meatloaf I ever had.

November 26

Had a great evening with Blackwell and Lamont kids (and a couple of Texas kids)—just what I needed to set my attitude back on track. Of course, cleaning up the *dog poop* that someone tracked into my house was not fun. It was, however, hilarious to watch him turn three shades of red when it happened.

I was thinking that I never took the time to get to know some of her friends. While I loved having kids over and liked the noise, the mess, the big feet, I really didn't know them as individuals. Since she has died, her friends have continued to come around and reveal themselves to me. In addition, at school and on Facebook, there are all these great kids letting me know that she is still present in their hearts and lives. I miss her so much. I wish she knew how much I love her friends and how they are honoring her by loving me back.

November 27

Some things never change, no matter the opportunity for growth, wisdom, second chances. Some things never change.

November 28

As we were leaving Walmart, Larry pointed out Venus in the western sky. The last time I was leaving Walmart, and he pointed out Venus, and we went home to a visit from the Oklahoma Highway Patrol. We did pretty good tonight at Walmart (it is typically a hard place for Emily and me). When we got home, there was a beautiful present from a high school friend who is also the wife of one of the paramedics who so valiantly fought for our Sarah.

November 30

Sometimes there are things that pop into my head and crowd out any capabilities I have of critical reasoning. Tonight, as I was talking to Mom, I told her that I never really got to know this one certain friend when Sarah was alive. She loved him so much and always talked about how fancy he was, and I just never took the time to recognize what a good kid he is. I wish I would have, and she could have known that I, too, think he is fancy—and more importantly, so does Granny.

There were kids in and out all the time, and I typically liked her friends, but I never realized what an exceptional individual he is. I knew several of her friends were really great, and they have lived up to what I would have expected had I ever imagine the twist my life path has taken. Every Tuesday night for a bit, he is here. Tonight Emily was retreating under her blanket with headphones when there was a knock at the door. I said, "Emily, he's here." She jumped up and said, "Is it Tuesday?!"

I wish Sarah could have known that I truly love him, and I get what she saw in him. He is remarkable.

Another thing that is haunting me is the last shopping trip the four of us took to Edmond/Oklahoma City for school clothes. I went shopping in this one store that I hated. It was really teeny-boppy, but she wanted some jewelry from there. I helped her pick it out, and she got really excited as we tried to find some coordinating pieces. I had given them each a dollar amount to spend, and she kept a close eye on not going over her amount.

After the mall and lunch, I wanted to stop at a store that I liked. She went in with me and picked out stuff for me to try on. I wound up getting nothing, but I remember her saying, "Mom?" at the dressing room door and having me step out to show her so she could give me her opinion.

Always about the clothes, never about my weird body shape. It was just me, the mom she loved, and it was her job to find me the perfect outfit. When I couldn't find anything, it wasn't that I was fat; it was that the store sucked. She was awesome like that.

That determined look on her little face as she checked sizes and held each piece up to other pieces to coordinate. I miss her so much.

December 3

I told her I loved her every day—several times a day in fact. But it still isn't enough.

I wish I could tell her one more time how crazy hip and cool I thought she was, how my heart would practically burst with pride at her tolerance and maturity, how from the moment I knew about her, I was wildly, passionately in love with her, and how now my heart aches every minute for her, how without her even the most beautiful things have a touch of ugliness to them, how sorry I am for the times I disappointed her, how I will miss her until the day I die.

I hope she is proud of us. Emily and I went to school all week. I didn't cry after going to Walmart today; I even walked by the brownie mix. I put up the Christmas tree. I plan to cook supper all week long.

I hope she isn't too disappointed that I still haven't gone into her room or even slept upstairs. Someday I will. Just not today.

And even though there is this huge gaping wound where my heart was, I hope she doesn't know about it and that she is at peace

December 10

Last night I was thinking about the man who was arrested for the murder of the girls in Weeletka. I am so glad that he will be held accountable. But I was struck by the fact that even if the families have answers and their killer is caught and brought to justice, the girls are. not. coming. back.

I fell asleep thinking about those families and how many questions they must have. I dreamed about Sarah (I always do now). And in my dream there were these three ladies who came to visit me. I was asleep on the couch, and they woke me and said they had some answers to my question. Right off the bat, they answered a big question for me. Then they took me to the accident scene and to the car. Neither were what I thought they would be. They took me to all the schools where I had taught to see the friends I had taught with and draw comfort from them. Then I got to talk to Sarah.

The bottom line is, even though answers do not bring back a dead child, they do bring a bit of peace. I decided this morning that I will be going to the accident scene and to see the car.

December 5

I am taking full advantage of this extra day. I used the leftover chicken from the Cornish game hens I cooked yesterday and made a chicken salad for lunch, put together a bacon cheeseburger meatloaf for tomorrow, and finished a pot of chili that I started soaking the beans for yesterday. Emily and I are cleaning house and then going shopping to pick up a few things for school this next week. Also, I taught Emily a crochet stitch last night (she now knows two stitches), and she is doing *amazing*. So, while we are out, we are getting her some yarn. It goes without saying that we miss Sarah terribly, but it felt good to cook all morning, Talked on the phone to Caroline to make our plans for the day, while Emily picked up the house and brought her project to me for me to help her turn to the next row. Today is a good day.

December 10

I am spent. Headache, heartache, tension body aches. Here was my day:

Woke up after dreaming about Sarah.

Wanted to see the car and accident site, but Mom showed me pictures instead. I think she was trying to control what I saw; there were no pictures of the inside of the car.

Went Christmas shopping for Sarah. She had money that she had given to Michael to hold for her. He brought it to us the day after she died, and I wanted to do something very special with that money. I used it to buy Caroline, Emily, Chanda, Justin, and Jenny (her sisters and brother), a Christmas present from Sarah. It was almost exactly enough to purchase for them what I wanted. I will post a picture of it after they all get them.

And then the shittiest part of the day: my purchase for Sarah? Not a book from Brace Books, not jewelry, not a pair of cool jeans from The Buckle or Twilight Woods from Bath and Body Works. No, I bought her a cross of poinsettias . . . for her grave.

Stupid freaking tire. Stupid freaking post

December 17

I just miss her so much. My life has become a series of days in which I can barely bear it and days in which I cannot bear it at all. Today was a not-bearing-it-at-all kind of day.

December 19

It seems like she was only here for a minute and has been gone for years.

December 21

Even in a comfortable evening, one little flash of her brings back sharpness.

She was so different.

Here was Sarah's birthday present to me and the reason for the precious tears that I have cried today. I was cleaning out the hope chest where I keep important papers, and I stumbled across a paper where she had written her mission statement after we read *The Six Most Important Decisions for Teens* by Covey. It was written in her own sweet penmanship, and even now I can hardly bear to read it. It is just so honest and true and profound and Sarah. I will never be the woman that she was.

> Sarah Virginia Ray's Life Mission Statement: *To be a good example to my younger sister, To graduate high school and college, To help who I can in whatever way I can, To love God, To change someone's life, To make a difference, To be a loving mother and wife one day, To be good enough to end up in Heaven.*

December 22

Thought it was impossible to love DCLA public schools and my friends anymore—that was before last night. I was quite tickled . . .

quite . . . by the hidden talents of my educator friends. After crying all day yesterday and wanting to be comatose until school starts back up, I have smiled several times today and even laughed out loud. Turns out, even after we turn forty, we still have the ability to be hip and cool, if only in the eyes of other forty-plus-year-olds. I think the younger ones all left early, but we older ones partied until at least *at least* 9:15 or 9:30.

I was also caught off guard by the nice cards, e-mails, texts, and messages on Facebook. Needless to say, I have aged more between forty and fort-one than I have previous birthdays, but the love and thoughtfulness of the people on my love chain has been—yet again—overwhelming.

Thank you for keeping our family in your prayers. In particular, please keep my brother in your prayers as he Christmases in Afghanistan.

Tonight is the night we opened Christmas presents and had our Christmas supper. I went to Starbucks and got everyone a nice coffee to drink while we opened presents. Then for supper I made sausage-spinach alfredo lasagna, tomato/mushroom gnocci, guacamole bruchetta, garlic bread, and vegetable dip.

December 25

On our way to Texas. We passed the site of the accident. It was my first time to see it. Skid marks are still there as is a bouquet of flowers. It seems like such a typical and nondescript place. Hard to fathom that something violent enough to take my brown-eyed daughter from me forever happened there.

December 27

Tonight as Larry and I were driving back from Texas, we came upon an accident that we are sure was a fatality accident. Because there were plenty of first responders there already, we didn't stop.

Needless to say, I became upset, and some of those ugly thoughts started swirling around my head.

One huge question that I have had but am unsure who to ask is this: Our church attendance was pretty sporadic over the years, Sarah had been saved, and we always did service to others projects, we discussed God frequently and we prayed, believed, and listened, but we did not attend church regularly.

Since she had passed, I have worried that I might have cost Sarah her heaven by not taking her to church regularly. Larry and I discussed this on the way home—if I was a good enough example for the girls. He reminded me of a time we went out to eat and I bought a cold man supper who had just come into Braum's to warm up. Sarah cried that night at Braum's—she was always so touched by the struggles of others and always wanted to lighten their burdens.

I just have this need to know that she is in heaven and that I didn't mess that up for her. I just always thought I would have more time, and I never could make a strong decision on whether or not organized religion was part of my belief system or not. I told Larry I thought I had shown her the acts of Christianity but was unsure that I had shown her enough of the biblical teachings for her to be in a state of grace (even though she had been be saved, which I guess is my answer).

I know that I am talking in circles and not very articulate. I just really am having a hard time getting my mind wrapped around the vastness of God's grace, heaven, and what we have to do to be worthy of it. It isn't like I can go marching up to God and demand a better grade in biology for her.

So I don't know where to go with these thoughts. I loved her and God loved her. She loved me and she loved God. I think we did God's work by loving and serving Him through blessing others. She had asked Jesus to be in her heart. I hope that was enough for her to go to heaven. She deserves to be there.

Caroline and I are going to start walking in the park. I remember there was this one summer that I walked in the park every day. One time she and Emily wore their rollerblades. One time she came and bounced a basketball all the way around the Fifth Street Park. We didn't talk much, just enjoyed the fall day, the quiet comfort that comes with knowing someone really, really well. I miss those unimportant times.

December 28

Oklahoma Department of Public Safety Report for September 2011. This is a cold faceless statistical report. Each of these numbers represents a loved one.

Department of Public Safety officials report a decrease in traffic fatalities for the month of September 2011. Fatalities were down by eleven in September with a total of 46 compared to 57 in the same month last year.

There were nine motorcyclist and zero pedestrians who died in crashes during September. The highest daily fatality numbers include 12 deaths on Fridays [Sarah died on a Friday], dropping to 10 on Sundays. There were eight deathless days in the month of September.

Four of the fatality crashes were alcohol-related, in the opinion of the investigating state, county or municipal officer [Sarah's accident was non-alcohol related]. Forty-two fatality victims were Oklahoma residents and four were nonresidents [Sarah was an Oklahoma resident]. There were 30 male and 15 female victims [Sarah was female].

Five of the fatality victims were age 20 or under [Sarah was 16]. Oklahoma County led the state in fatalities with a fatality count of eight, followed by Tulsa with four fatalities each [Sarah died in Noble County].

The highest number of fatality crashes was on State Highways with 16. There were 13 fatalities on County Roads [Sarah's accident happened on an interstate].

Forty-five percent of those who died in traffic collisions were not wearing safety belts at the time of the crash, according to DPS statistics [we do not know if she was wearing her seatbelt].

Year to date fatalities through October 10, 2011-524. [She is one of these souls.]

January 1

I saw a picture of her peeking out of the swimming pool. The sun was in her eyes, and she was smiling. Her hair was matted to her head. She loved the sun and summer and heat. We had spent a lot of time outside this summer. I mowing; she or Emily bringing me drinks. Me in the pool; her jumping into the pool in her bra and shorts, stating that it covered more than her bathing suit. Emily would have never done that—me either. That was something great about her—so spontaneous, free spirited. Sometimes she would just sit on the top step or Emily would, and we would chat as I floated around. I loved it after dark. Me floating in the dark, the girls on the pool edge or patio chatting.

She is everywhere . . . and nowhere. I found one of her school papers tonight—in her sweet left-handed penmanship (which was quite lovely for a lefty). One day the last week she had told me about a friend who was going to high school online and how she liked the way the program was set up (the computer program—the way the actual software worked). She described in detail how the user could take notes with the program open and how the testing system worked.

I haven't written on my projects in a while. I often had her read over my stuff or talk to me about it. I wonder if I ever will write again for pleasure rather than necessity.

Today I found a no-fiction article on the topic on which I based a project. Kind of encouraged me. I know that I have to finish my project. Not because she would want me too (she would), but because I want to.

I am so proud of Caroline and Emily. They have forged ahead with a healthy and loving relationship.

Today Emily came to my class only to grab a notebook today and look for her sociology book.

I was digging out my other coat and came across my old long sweater. I had two of them, and they were both red. She would wear them around the house like a robe. They would absolutely swallow her. She would get in bed with me and curl up with her butt in the air, her legs under her, like a baby and say, "Hi!" in this really silly, cheerful voice. She was really swell.

January 3

Seventeen years ago tonight, I started feeling the twinges of labor, even though I was going to be induced in the morning. The following morning, I arrived at the hospital dilated to a three centimeters. About six hours later, I had a beautiful little girl. She had a nice round head, tons of hair (even on her back), and was *fat*. Her eyes were very dark, and I knew that they would turn brown (which they did very quickly). She spent some time in the NICU because she struggled to breathe initially. After a few hours, they brought her to us, and she was perfect.

I held her as I slept. And over the years, she and I spent a lot of nights together. Sometimes all four of us girls would pile in one bed and fall asleep watching movies or chatting. I miss that falling asleep all crowded and snuggled.

When we left the hospital, Lisa and I took her to my mom's shop. Mom promptly painted her tiny fingernails red. After she passed away, Aunt Karmen painted her fingernails red.

She was perfectly Sarah for sixteen years and seven months.

Today, as Emily and I were driving to school, a rocking chair sat on the roadside. We both just looked at it and looked at each other as if to say, "Was that a . . . nah . . . it couldn't be a . . . rocking chair?" It was in pretty rough shape, and I thought back to a torn dollar. Sarah had said that just because it was damaged didn't mean it had no worth. She wouldn't let me throw it away and was going to tape it back together. After she died, I found that torn dollar in her backpack. I think it had become a metaphor for her life. She felt so damaged from the years of depression and poor health. But she still had a great deal of worth. DCLA was the tape that was putting her back together. She was so happy those last weeks and days and even hours of her life.

If she were here, tomorrow she would be getting a pair of Buckle jeans, some cash, probably some jewelry or purse or perfume. She would have a few pals over for a movie and some cake. Our birthdays were always very low key.

Instead, we are going to design and order her headstone. I don't know all the details of what will be on it. I just know it will be *fancy*. Emily has arranged for us to go to the lake at dusk, where we always had our July 4th celebration, and release balloons with letters to her. Larry asked her if she wanted to do it at the cemetery. Emily told him that is not where Sarah is.

I never mention Sarah at school, but respond cheerfully and honestly when the kids ask about her. Today, as we were waiting for the bus driver to come, we were standing by the door, looking out. One of my friends asked, "Where is Sarah? I just miss her." Another friend said, "Don't you remember? First she got killed in a car wreck. Then she died. Now she is in heaven."

Yep.

January 3—Evening

Just told Sarah happy birthday. Right after, I heard the song "Umbrella" that she danced to on the video.

January 4

Me: "I will be gone this afternoon. Today is Sarah's birthday, and Emily is having a bit of a bad day. Also, I have to take care of business. Do you know what a headstone is?"

Kids: "Yeah." (One student said that a relative had one.)

Me: "It is a very special stone that goes on the grave that has the name of a person on it. We are going to pick out and order a headstone for Sarah."

Student 1: "I thought she was up there" (points to sky).

Student 2: "She is. It is for her grave."

Student 1: "Why are you getting her a birthday present if she is . . . up there?" (points to sky again).

Me: "We are going today because Caroline and Granny are off work today, and they want to help pick it out . . . not because it is her birthday."

Student 1 still didn't seem think the idea of getting a headstone for your birthday would be a good gift. I agree with him.

Friend 1: "Happy birthday, Emily."

Friend 2: "It isn't Emily's birthday; it is Sarah's."

Friend 1: "But I can't tell Sarah happy birthday."

Friend 2: "Oh yeah. I forgot that part."

January 6

One time Sarah and I were watching an episode of *Roseanne*. There is one scene where Jackie gets mad at Roseanne and tells her, "There is a really easy way to tell us apart. You. Me." And while she is saying "you," she whirls her palms around Roseanne's face. When she says "me," she swirls her palms around her own face. Sarah and I would do that to each other at random times and then die laughing.

She also loved quotes. Sometimes I would read a quote to her, and Emily and they would both yell, "Facebook dibs!" One that they both thought was hilarious was, "Why don't you eat some makeup so you will be pretty on the inside too. Silly girls. Tonight Emily and I came across a quote that we both thought was hilarious: Sisters are like fat thighs; they stick together.

January 9

She is so far away. Bad, bad, very bad night.

January 15

She loved *What's Eating Gilbert Grape*. When she was younger, she sometimes wore flip-flops that were too big for her. She was never afraid of hard, sweaty work—in fact, she liked to work in the garden, mow, paint, and that sort of thing as opposed to housework. She preferred fruit to junk food, but sometimes she would eat a whole candy bar and drink a pop very fast.

January 16

I don't remember her voice.

Larry and I went shopping this evening and then takeout and home.

I was just sitting in the living room and thought what it was like when she would take a shower or bath in the evening. She had this huge, yellow, soft sweatshirt that she got when she was in fifth grade. She had spilled something on her shirt before school, and my friend—the site-based social worker—had this shirt in her office. Sarah had changed into that day, loved it, and my friend told her to keep it. It had become so worn and ragged and soft. She would put on that huge sweatshirt after bathing and wear it around the house with her hair pulled up in a messy bun. For some reason I can just see her standing in the kitchen in that sweatshirt, licking a spoon, and then coming into the living room to sit in her chair or on the couch with her legs all folded up under her.

Sarah was one of those people who literally chose every day to be in a good mood. It was so hard for her to push aside doubt and depression and insecurity and low self-worth to be who the world saw. The evenings were good for her. She loved the night, and she would just be so relaxed in the evenings—sitting on the porch for a while no matter how hot or cold it was outside, eating some fresh fruit—her snack of choice. (I no longer even go to that section, and there's no need for apples in our house anymore.) She'd text or write there. I think that sometimes it is not the things that I want to talk to her about that I miss or the trips or shopping or new movies, but just the hanging out. Just her presence.

I told Mom today that sometimes it is easier to miss her than it was to worry about her—about her health, her mental health, her future. I know that nothing bothers her now. I am the one hurting now, not both of us. She breathes deeply and without tightness; she has no stomach ulcers and pain; she sees herself through God's eyes and knows how beautiful and worthy she is and always was.

I dream about her and my dad. In my dreams, Dad usually does all the talking, but she is being a helpmate to him, just like she always was to whoever needed her. She is always with him in my dreams, and smiling, but silent.

I miss her laugh. I miss her voice. I miss her.

January 19

After dealing with some ridiculousness, Emily and I took a moment to visit Sarah's resting place after school. Sometimes, lately, I feel unsure of what my next step should be. When I take the time to reflect and think, the answer comes through loud and clear. My life has always been about doing what is best for my kids. That hasn't changed. How do I best help Emily? What does Caroline need? How do I best advocate for Sarah? Hands down and gloves off, my girls are my driving force.

January 23

Today my pussycat has been gone for four months. The coincidences amaze me. I checked the mail, and the mockup of her stone was in the mail. It needs to be tweaked just a bit. I am not sure the words to the hymn are correct. I always sang it another way. But that could be like the kid who sang the song about the "Donzer Lee Light" ("The Star Spangled Banner").

The last four months seem like one big block of time. Here is my life with Sarah:

- Before Sarah—Day one.
- Sarah as a baby—Day two.
- Sarah in elementary school reading all the time, winning reading and writing contests, and laughing—Day three.
- Sarah after eighth grade, when the self-loathing and the tears and the darkness started—Day four.
- My last summer with Sarah with her sitting on the edge of the pool or jumping in with her bra and cutoffs, chatting with me—Day five.
- Sarah at Lamont, when we saw our old Sarah reemerging—Day six.
- The night Sarah died—Day seven (lasted ten years).
- The week after Sarah died—Day eight (also lasted ten years).
- The next three months and three weeks—Day nine.

So many things have changed in the last four months. I am twenty years older than I was four months ago. I believe more strongly in God and His sweet blessings than I did four months ago. I don't cry as often as I did four months ago, but it is much more soul-wrenching when I do. Heaven is closer than it was four months ago . . . because Sarah is there. I dream more than I did four months ago. I doubt my effectiveness as a parent more than I did four months ago. A huge portion of me and who I was four months ago is gone.

Some things have stayed the same in the last four months. I am still Caroline's mom and Emily's mom—and Sarah's mom. I am still blessed to have a job that I cherish every day. I am still the daughter of a strong and voracious woman who has taught me (by example) how to live life with a bulldog tenacity *and* how to be a lady. I still have a lot of love and guidance left to give to my kids. And although a huge portion of me and who I was is gone, a huge portion of me and who I will become lingers.

Even when I am distracted and my conscious self isn't missing her every minute, my heart is. Sarah and her sisters and lovelovelovelove is the first thing on my mind before I even open my eyes in the morning, and it is the last thing I think of as I drift off and my dreams begin. While there is a lasting heaviness setting in, there is also a conflicting temporary feeling to the pain. I have never felt the faith in heaven and reunification that I do now. I am tired and sad and heavy hearted, but I am hopeful and ephemeral and surrounded.

January 23

At this moment four months ago, my child lay in a car fighting for her life as a nurse was stopping to help her in her fight. If was a futile fight, as were the efforts of the paramedics and emergency room personnel. No amount of knowledge, equipment, or technology would save her. The only thing that would have saved her that night was a tire that hadn't been shoddily manufactured.

January 24

Dammit—"One Sweet Day."

January 25

September 23, 2011, I suffered one of the great heartbreaks of my life. September 26, 2012, what will be one of my greatest joys is due.

February 1

My heart hurts today. So much.

February 3

I thought this morning, as I was digging through my drawers for a pair of trouser socks, of a morning that we were all racing around trying to get ready. I called up the stairs to Sarah to grab me a pair of pantyhose. She came down with one knee-high and said, "Mom, I could only find one panty ho." I miss those moments of hilarity and quick wit of hers. And I miss how easy laughter used to come. I smiled with that memory this morning. But I miss laughing.

February 5

This was the roughest week I have had in a while. Thank goodness for a super replenishing weekend.

Every second of every minute of every hour of every day there is a profound sadness in my heart. Even when I am not thinking about her, there is a longing for her. But here and there I am finding joy and humor. There are things I still cannot face, still cannot think on, things I cannot speak of. But I have stumbled across a couple of pieces of myself.

I think the part that is Sarah's mom will always have moments of panic, like when I opened her bedroom door for the first time in a long time today. Her purse was lying open like she had just come home and left it there. I almost expected to hear her popping open a Dr Pepper.

She has been my welcome company at night as I dream of her almost every night. But the dreams have been very different than my usual vivid, colorful, and noisy dreams. Not bad dreams, just very black and white and foggy—and silent and filled with Sarah. I haven't dreamed of her in the last couple of nights, and I have slept well and awakened with very mixed heart pangs. Rested and more focused on the day at hand, but tender-sore hearted.

I did a lot of cooking this weekend, spent time with Mom, talked about baby things, cleaned, made a baby outfit, painted a canvas, went on a date, planned a menu and got groceries, and had the Big Em all to myself for a while. All of the things I love. Except Sarah. Forevermore, it will be except Sarah.

February 11

Some other great things happened today. My heart has been trying to work up to a crying jag for a couple of days. There are several people who God put in my path to bring me cheer today.

I bumped into two sweet gals that are the very best of friends. They were overjoyed to see me and hugged me. One of them told me that I was awesome and great and pretty and funny and strong (who doesn't need to hear that from an enthusiastic person). They both held me twice and had me laughing as I walked away.

I bumped into a friend, who discussed baby names with me. I saw another mom of a heavenly daughter that I had been needing to thank her for something she wrote to me that has gotten me through many a day. I saw not one, not two or three, but four teacher friends.

People matter. Things don't.

February 13

Hey, Mr. Dependable loser, perhaps you should spend less time building doofy-looking snowmen and more time making sure the product leaving your business isn't going to kill someone. Shyster.

Growing pains.

February 14

"Ma'am, I need you to talk to me."

February 15

Last night was bad, bad, very bad. Mom has had a rough few days, and in talking to her last night, the combination of worry for her and the excitement for Baby Hadley and the joy of Emily and taking care of some of Sarah's business . . . I guess I just became very overwrought. I had this great day and nice evening, and then there was this onslaught of grief, and I was sobbing uncontrollably.

I never know when it is going to hit me, but it is always in the evening and always at home (fortunately). I went through my missing Sarah routine—pacing around the house, crying, hugging myself, and wringing my hands.

I go sit on the back porch—not sure why I feel so close to her there. I tell her how sorry I am and how much I miss her. I pray for a little peace. There have been three times now that this has been my unintended routine. There have been three times that I have had a genuine physical reaction to prayer. It is as if someone pours a pitcher of warm water over me, so soothing and relaxing. A big sigh and loosening of muscles. I sniffle, wipe my eyes, and wipe the dog kisses off me. (Rachel and Luke really are concerned when all this is going on. After I tell them that it doesn't help, they just lie down beside me.)

Mom told me that she thought Sarah was worth missing. That she wouldn't trade the sixteen years we had with her for anything. And I agree. Sarah had hurt for so long. It is so painful to see our kids hurting or struggling. We would do anything for them—to make it better. As parents we often tell our children that we would take their pain if we could. I get to do that. I get to shoulder the pain for the rest of my life—but Sarah is pain free. So I guess, in a way, I have taken her pain for her, and that is a cool thing.

February 17

I got a maternity pattern for a nice summer shirt for Caroline. I am going to make a few of them for her. Also a couple of shorts and skirts and capris. Going to make them over the next few weekends.

Caroline is pregnant like I was pregnant with her and like Mom was pregnant with me. *Sick* and *tired*. She has lost seven pounds with no end in sight. She throws up everything. We have her on ginger ale, and today she ate some grapes that tasted good to her. She comes over every evening and sleeps. The day is just too long for her body that is working so hard to make me a grandchild. I lost twenty-five pounds when I was pregnant with her. I was so miserable for nine months, and I think that it will be a long nine months for her.

Mitch has a feeling in his gut that it is a girl. We all kind of have that feeling (not that we care). I am really proud of Mitch; he is already talking and acting like a dad. Making sacrifices and decisions like a dad would. A *good* dad. I can't wait to see him hold his baby. His grandma did a great job raising him.

Emily and I were talking the other day about when the little one is big enough to say, "Aunt Em, take me for ice cream." She just beamed. She is going to be the hip and cool aunt who really "gets" the kids when the ridiculously unfair parents do not.

Nicholas doesn't like babies, so he isn't saying much about it. He has decided he will sit by stinky Emily at the basketball game, but is not budging on sharing popcorn with her. I cannot imagine the difference between this last Christmas when he asked where Sarah was and this next Christmas, with the baby here.

All I can do is smile when I think about that baby. *That baby*! Can you believe it? A. baby. is. coming.

February 20

I have been really working on my attitude this evening. I am really worried about my mom. Ronnie comes home (well, stateside anyway) in a few days, and she is worried about him. She has really struggled with missing Sarah for a few days. We are trying to get Caroline and Mitch moved, which has meant a tremendous amount of work on the house. I could've been a better teacher today. Poor me. Blah, blah blah . . .

So I have been really trying to find something to be happy about, and I just happened across something on the Internet that *totally* turned my day around.

It was a picture of Tom Selleck. He is so damn sexy. I think I shall print that picture off. Mmmm, yummy.

February 21

Me: "Boys and girls, I am leaving a bit early today, because I have to take care of some business for Sarah. But I will be back first thing in the morning."

Friend: "Does Mr. Desbien know that you are getting married?"

Me: [Blank stare]

Rough afternoon. We had to take care of some legal business concerning Sarah, and that always halts my "getting better" with screaming, screeching brakes. She is always *always* with us, but focusing on the accident and her death (rather than her and who she was) is ridiculously painful. So, after that crappy experience,

I followed some good advice (to get happy in the same pants I got crappy in) and had a little Hobby Lobby therapy, Spencer therapy, and cooking therapy. Much better. Head, neck, back, shoulders are much, *much* better.

Emily and I cooked for pool league tonight, and Mitch and Caroline loaded it up in the car. The teams take turns bringing food, and I am in week two of a three-week stretch of cooking for the league. I try out new experiments on them, and I have had mad, crazy success (using other people's recipes). I love cooking for people and trying out new recipes. Tonight's recipes were all from *Taste of Home* and were *wonderful*.

Tonight I made

- sweet and sour meatballs (about fist sized); thumbs up!
- bacon-wrapped water chestnuts with homemade barbecue sauce; thumbs *way up*!
- southern corn salad; thumbs down for the bar crowd, but it would be perfect to take on a picnic
- gourmet potato soup with sautéed mushrooms, onions, garlic, and bacon; thumbs up!

February 23

Five months ago was both yesterday—and a lifetime ago.

February 24

First time to eat at Hunan's since Sarah. She always filled her plate with fried rice, red sauce, and cocktail shrimp. We would leave with this huge pile of shrimp skin on the table. She was such a freak!

February 25

We went to the Beatles review "Liverpool Legends" tonight. It was unbelievable. If you ever have the chance to see one of these shows, don't pass it up. They were incredible musicians and showmen.

They played "Imagine" by John Lennon, which was one of Sarah's favorite songs and was played at her funeral. I just closed my eyes and let the tears flow. Emily said, "Mom *look*!" I opened my eyes, and there on the big screen was a peace sign. It was purple.

Is it kind, necessary, or right? I try to think of this before I act, but I gotta tell you, *every time* I drive by that ridiculous-looking "Dependable" business (the one that doesn't know its product well enough to keep folks safe), I give it the finger.

February 26

Watching *I Survived*. This week is about people who died and went "to the white light." It is strangely comforting.

February 28

Because I gave my plot to Sarah, I bought another one today. Couldn't get the one right next to her, but there will just be one person between us. She is right next to Uncle Doc and about four down from my dad. Relieved to have that done.

Haunted.

February 29

She is still here. I am still her mom. Her body may have been damaged beyond repair, but her soul wasn't. The love remains.

Making a quick run to Edmond with Mom. I heard a sniffle from the back seat and turned to look at Emily. (She has a cold.) She was looking out the window so deep in thought. The sun was shining right in her eyes. I have never seen her eyes look so turquoise.

March 3

If you are buying tires from someone who handles used tires, please make sure that you are buying from a reputable dealer. Even if they advertise themselves as being "dependable," they may not be. In the words of an old TV ad, "There is a lot riding on your tires."

March 4

:(

March 5

Spent the day with Caroline and Emily. Even though I was looking forward to it and we had planned it weeks ago, I spent most of the day missing Sarah. We got several pair of the cheap flip-flops at Old Navy, and the girl said something about us needing so many because there were three of us. I suppose there will come a day when I will settle into it being just the three of us instead of the four of us girls. But that day was not today. Every day there is a long shadow that falls on everything I do. I suppose there will come a day when the shadow will be shorter and not so dark, and I will see more of the sunshine that I know is still there. But, again, that day was not today.

Starting to feel better. It has been a rough few days. Mom cut my hair. I finished a Service to Others project, got some comfort food in my tummy, made an overdue doctor's appointment, and worked outside this evening. Sometimes peace doesn't find me, I have to find it myself.

March 6

Emily sang on the way home today. She ran into the house and locked me out, laughing. She is watching *Ridiculousness* and giggling to herself. She had a spirited debate earlier this evening about politics. She ate all her supper. She is reading. Today was a great day!

March 15

Went to Sarah's grave today. I never know when I am going. I had a great day, but about halfway home I found myself thinking about her and her little books when she was little. She always loved to read. I was thinking about her little haircut at that age. She was so stinking cute. I don't know what induces the sudden tears, but today, on the way home, it was just like someone flipped a switch.

When I got to the cemetery, I cried and sang "The Pussycat Song" to her that I sang to her all the time. I sat there for a long time. I told her I loved her and that I missed her and Granny missed her and Emily and Caroline missed her and that she was going to be an aunt and that I was sorry for my shortcomings as a mom and that she deserved better and I looked at the things people have put on her grave. After a while, there was a breeze on my face. For some reason, I always think the breeze is her. Then I left her there.

They say God never gives me more than I can handle. I used to take comfort in that, because I knew I was weak and assumed God knew this too. Today I decided that either He has grossly overestimated me, or I have grossly underestimated me.

March 21

I am *beyond* furious. I need a sledgehammer and a *bunch* of stuff to mess up.

Today Mom met with the investigators, and they all went to the scene of the accident and to the car (which I now own). Mom said there was a lot of blood in the back seat where she was, and she also found Sarah's shorts and her purple shoes that she was wearing.

I also found out the name of the tire. It was sold at a used tire dealer here in Ponca who has no record of where it came from. There was a recall on this brand of tire, although I do not know if the year this tire was made was effected.

It is just infuriating that something as critical as a tire would ever *ever* have to be recalled for a manufactured defect. I want to know why my child was in a car with that shitty tire on it. I want to know why she is lying out there in that cemetery instead of here with me, reading or shuffling or sitting on the front porch. I want to know why she will never see Caroline's baby or Emily without her braces next month. I want to know why the boy driving will have to live forever with what he saw that night and the nightmare of having to face me the next day. I want to know if the cheapness of the tire and the profit the dealer made from it were worth it. Money may make the world go around, but it stopped mine.

March 22

I have Nutella and graham crackers and a butter knife, and you don't. Take that, freaking Cooper Tires.

March 26

Things Sarah missed:

1. Highway 60 being completed.
2. The earthquake that knocked my sign off the wall and scared the crap out of me. (I thought a train was coming through the house.)
3. Nutella, my new discovery. She would have melted.
4. The senior boys walking around with their baby dolls in the doll carriers today (even coming in from track practice, which the babies attended). And the one senior who got a threat to call DHS because he left his baby in the pickup. Though he did leave the truck running, so the baby wouldn't be hot.
5. Emily saying today that when the freshmen get the babies next week, she is naming it Natalie Faye, since that is what Sarah was going to name her daughter.
6. The new awesome DCLA track shirts that honor Sarah.
7. Caroline and Mitch turning into a family (I think they are more in love now than they ever have been).

8. Seeing Allison Krause live.

9. Emily developing a strong interest in what may be her life passion.
10. Her mother at donkey basketball (Lord, have mercy).
11. Her granny teaching people how to do the Stroll.
12. Today and tomorrow and all the rest of the days.

However, I read somewhere that when we experience pain in our life, it is like a black thread in our life tapestry. We are looking at the tapestry from the bottom and see all the loose ends and the starts and stops and the ugly black thread. But after we die and go to heaven, we get to see the tapestry from the top and see just what the Master Stitcher was making for us. From our new point of view, we see that the black thread was just what the tapestry needed to make it beautiful. So although she is missing earthly things that I wish she was here to share, I know that she is standing in awe of her life tapestry.

March 26

„Ba, da, da, da, da, da, da, da, da, da, da, da. All . . . my . . . friends . . . drive a low rider."

We were going to school one morning, and this song came on the radio. She and Emily screamed, and we turned the radio up *really* loud. We loved to watch George Lopez. Sometimes we would say to each other, "Oh *no* you *di*-ent."

I love to remember stuff like that.

April 1

Turns out that when I am really dreading an upcoming day (like a beautiful spring prom day that will not find my brown-eyed daughter getting her hair fancied up and wearing a fancy dress, with a fancy guy), I can take enough allergy medicine to just sleep through the day.

But here is the rub: I also miss a day of looking forward to my grandchild coming, sitting on the porch with my mother, working in the flowerbeds with my daughters, sharing a meal or a project with Larry, baking cookies for Mitch, talking to friends, creating art, making up some amazing new recipe, working on my mission, drinking ice tea, doing a crossword puzzle, or any of the hundreds of other blessings I still have.

April 2

Her stone has been set. I have no words, other than I love her and feel her love as much as I ever did. And I miss her more than I ever thought it possible to miss anyone. She was a great human being, and my world will always be a little dimmer without her in it.

Believe it or not, I am relieved to have the stone in place. It is the last present I will ever purchase for her. And it is beautiful.

I always associate a breeze on my face with her presence. When I got out of the car, I left the door open and strode across the graveyard until I reached her place. I sat down on the ground and cried a while. Then the breeze blew across my face, and I instantly felt better. I don't know why that makes me think she is near. But, it always, *always* rests my soul. I think I seek that gentle breeze, because when that yucky old grief sneaks up on me, I inadvertently wind up outside, in one of her two spots. And it usually goes the same way each time: I cry for a while, the breeze blows on my face, I feel better.

So I dusted the stone off a bit, ran my fingers on her name, and looked at the picture. Emily was excited to see it, so she was taking pictures as my mom and Charles arrived. Just a few minutes later, Caroline and Mitch and Baby Hadley came, and Chanda and Nicholas came right behind them. We took quite a few pictures and told some funny stories. Emily's electronic baby from science started crying, so we were laughing about that. Nicholas found a random silk flower on the ground and went off in search of a grave with no flowers to put it on.

And it almost felt normal, until we left without her . . . again.

March 3

Sometimes, in the heat of the moment, we say things we don't mean. Sometimes we say things we mean, but lack the maturity to understand any life truths other than our own. Sometimes we just stick our foot in our mouth. I think that last night and today there was a lot of each of these happening on Facebook concerning Sarah. Someone tagged a picture of her on a friend's wall with an unfortunate slur. It was unfortunate because it hurt a lot of people, angered a lot of people, saddened a lot of people. I don't know what the truth is concerning who tagged it, who allowed the tag, who took care of it, but I would like for us all to give each other the benefit of the doubt and a little forgiveness and a little grace. Not because that is what Sarah would have wanted, but because it is the right thing. We cannot move forward to our mission when we are mired in anger and defense and comebacks.

March 5

A friend hearing me laugh at a funny video we watched on YouTube: "Teacher, I *love* your laugh."

March 6

Family.

March 9

I feel like I hear Him louder now that at any other time in my life. I *know* I feel His presence more now.

March 10

Three months before Sarah was killed, the owner of the car she was in purchased a tire from someone who bills himself as being "dependable." At the time of the purchase, the owner of the car was assured that the tire would be a good tire. Three months later, my child was lying in a morgue. The investigators of the accident, who specialize in tire safety, sent me a notification that the tire was "very used, rotten, and should have been in a trash pile." I don't know a lot about tires, but I do know what *dependable* means.

March 11

I am so thankful that I have Mrs. Black and Mrs. Schuermann and my sweet little friends' families so that I can fall apart if I need to. I have done so good as far as not missing any school for psychotic breaks since Christmas, and this one just kind of snuck up on me. I texted Mrs. Black and a student's mothers last night at ten. The mom assured me it would be fine for me to continue my nervous breakdown. This morning Mrs. Black texted me at six and told me they would be fine. Mrs. Schuermann came in on her day off. I could not ask for more from two ladies. They give me the love and support that allows me to parent Sarah the only way that I can at this point.

I dreamed about Sarah last night. I hadn't dreamed of her in a long time, and I was so confused when I went to bed as to what was the right way to move forward. In my dream, she was younger, about twelve or thirteen. She and I were together, and someone (wondering which of my daughters she was) asked her, "Now, which one are you?" Sarah said, "I am the pretty one . . . and the funny one . . . and the smart one." Then she laughed. I hadn't heard her laugh in such a long time. It was a sweet dream.

It is amazing to me how far laughter goes in soothing anger and raw hearts.

March 15

Yesterday I did nothing but homework and paperwork and recliner work and TV work. This has become my Saturday habit—to be comatose and not deal with anything but my heart and remembering. It is always a very quiet day. I make deals with myself through the week that if I be good, I can fall apart on Saturday. It is kind of my rebellion against the world. You take my kid; I don't deal with you for one whole day.

Today I have cleaned house, unloaded the dishwasher, cleaned the litter box, gotten a roast going, put together a meatloaf for tomorrow, made Emily a list of groceries to purchase (and I think she may have taken slightly more money than the groceries will come to—hmmm), baked a batch of cookies, made chili for chili brats on Tuesday, and made plans to make a treat for my coworkers later today. If the sun comes out, I may even mow. I am doing what has become my typical Sunday stuff. Cooking, cleaning, smiling, thinking to the future.

My goal for this week is to have a productive Saturday as well as Sunday. There are lots of things to be done in my life mission that could be accomplished during this wasted day each week. Not sure what kind of deal I will have to make with myself to get through the week, but I have to stop my maudlin Saturdays.

I have a big hurdle coming up in one month. That is when I will say "so long" to the little friends who saved my life. I would not have been able to get out of bed in the mornings had I not had them to go to. My classroom was a place I was amused, loved, and taught by these remarkable and compassionate little people. Not sure what my summer will be like, but I am making some plans to work on my classroom and my house. We are going to take a weekend trip or two. Lots of swimming and getting ready for baby. And I am sure bouts of tears and aching. But before I know it, I will be meeting new little friends and Little Hadley (who I pray to God has its father's disposition).

Onward.

When Sarah died, people said that it could have been so much worse; I don't think they intended to minimize my suffering, just stating that we were still very blessed. I just read online that the three children who died in yesterday's tornado in Woodward were sisters. I was absolutely stunned to read that. I am just shocked and devastated for their mother.

April 17

Our accountant tried to file our taxes online. Turns out someone has used Sarah's name and Social Security number as a dependent. I certainly hope it is a mistake and not what it could be.

I had a big old fit, paced around outside, called my mom. *But* who has two thumbs and didn't cry or go home? This girl!

April 18

Hey, tax frauder and shyster tire man, I have Nutella and graham crackers, and you don't. Go, me!

April 21

Who has two thumbs, has gotten things accomplished, and isn't having a maudlin Saturday? This gal!

April 23

She is another month away. Seven months.

Nights are the worst. In the beginning of Life After Sarah, the mornings were the worst. At the time, I didn't form the thought that I was facing a day without her, but now I realize that must have been what I was doing. Now the mornings are more hopeful than other times of the day. Mornings mean lists of things to do, the newspaper, meals to prepare, maybe the lawn needing to be mowed, trash to be taken out. And there is a sense of accomplishment and ruggedness and satisfaction in those things. But at night there is nothing; everyone is asleep, I cannot wake Larry up, call Mom, drive to Sonic, sit on the porch. It is just me and the chasm of missing Sarah.

Of my three daughters, she was the only night owl like me. We loved the night. Often this time of night would find us both still awake, watching TV, doing puzzles, reading, talking, computering, or just being. Now I do those things alone, and there is an emptiness to every night thing. And a sharpness to the grieving. I do not allow myself to lie in bed awake. My mind wanders to the cemetery, to her grave, to her casket, to my dead child, and I cannot bear it—the morbidity of it all.

Her telling me she wasn't going to the prom and us arguing over it. (She said it wasn't important to her. Did she know?) That week before she died, she was awake all night long for two nights, including the night before she died. It seems almost surreal remembering that last night, the driving lesson, me being sick, and her having her hand on my back, her staying up all night rocking, us talking and her listening to music—almost as if she was trying to soak up every last minute she had here.

So I putter around until I am sleepy and exhausted and fall into bed and go directly to sleep. No reading in bed or puzzle books or thinking—just sleep. Very primitive and functional sleep, not for leisure or replenishment. Just for survival.

I remember the day I realized that she had been gone a week. Seven days. I was almost relieved, thinking that I had done so well for seven days: stayed busy, remained positive, focused on other things. Like I did when she was away traveling and I knew she would be home soon. I was unloading the dryer on day seven, and I came across her shirt, and I cried into it, realizing that there was no end to this journey. She wouldn't be returning with a backpack full of dirty clothes and change and bobby pins.

And now we are at seven months. She is seven months away, and every day I get a little more resigned to the fact that she is moving further and further away from me in time.

April 24

Much better night tonight than last night. Very settled and comfortable tonight. It is amazing what being with people does for me.

Sugar and spice and everything nice

Sunshine and rainbows and ribbons for hair bows

Tea parties, laces and baby doll faces

that's what little girls are made of

April 30

Well, guess who still cannot go into her daughter's room without having a hot mess of a crying jag? Maybe another day.

I went in to look for a missing TV cable. Larry had tried to go in today to get the cable and just closed the door and came back out. I knew that when I opened the door, her purse would be lying there open on her table and that would set me off like it always does. It just looks like she has come home and dropped it there. So I opened the door, went straight to the table, and put the purse in her closet.

Her room is a mess. We just brought the stuff from her funeral and set it in there. There is the flyer from the casket we purchased, all the stuff from the funeral home, her backpack, her purse, her guitar, her pictures, her canvases.

Quite some time ago, I asked Larry to take her medicine out of the medicine cabinet and put it somewhere else. I couldn't bear to look at it when I went to get Tylenol or Benadryl. The box of her medicine is in her room.

I found her journal. Some very profound writing. I will share it someday, but that will also have to come another day.

We still have no idea where the TV cable is.

May 2

My brother told me when I could not find Sarah's class ring that God had it stored away and was saving it for me for when I needed it. I think that was the case with a text that I received tonight that was sent on November 3, by one of the ER nurses who worked on Sarah the night she needed so much love and help. While they were not able to save her, they did love her that night and fought for her, and helped her as much as humanly possible and went way above and beyond the call of duty. It amazes me that I can feel such love and respect for people I have never met and who glided into my life on the worse night of my life. Love is a strange little beast. I find it in the most unexpected places.

May 4

It does not matter what you have gone through in the last year or how much you have done for someone, if she has four legs and barks, she will take a giant dump on the last strip you have to mow. Thanks, Lydia. Really. You are never using my conditioner again.

May 9

Some days, it is easier to miss her than it was to worry about her. Today is not one of those days.

Tonight was a very special night. Emily got to stand up for being a football manager. The track coach called us to the front when they were awarding medals to the team and awarded us a state champion medal for Sarah. Not a lot of dry eyes. In the slide show was a picture of Emily and a picture of the Sarah Smiles purple banner that the team ran through at the football game. Very special evening with very special people. I cannot say how much I love DCLA and love the people of Deer Creek and Lamont. Chad Hutchinson, David Zachary, and Michael Thompson are amazing coaches and men of integrity. *And* the kids—also an amazing group of individuals.

May 11

Made the hard decision of who would receive the 2012 Sarah Virginia Ray Fancy Memorial Scholarship. We will be giving it every year, and I hope in future years it will not be so hard to choose. After reading and rereading the applications and thinking about each kid and who Sarah was, we came to a decision that I am proud of, although several of the men and women graduating tonight would have made a deserving honoree.

> *We struggled long and hard with the decision of who would receive the very first Sarah Virginia Ray Fancy Memorial Scholarship. We knew that the person we chose would have to be someone very special. However, we never anticipated that the group of individuals would be so talented and have such bright futures. Every application we read made the selection process harder and harder.*

> *The person we chose is someone who conducts themselves with quiet dignity and a humble spirit.*

> *Sarah always saw the world through a different lens and wanted everyone to see the world differently. To Sarah, the world was a place that needed more for those who had less, peace for those who lived in turmoil, warmth for those who knew indifference. It is ironic that Sarah saw the world through different eyes, and we have chosen a future optometrist to receive a scholarship in her name.*

> *The person that we have chosen to receive the Sarah Virginia Ray Fancy Memorial Scholarship is Andrew Coufal.*

One thing I forgot to say about graduation: all the men graduating had on purple shirts and ties tonight.

May 13

How do I possibly thank my mom for everything? There are not enough English words to let her know what my heart feels for her. I know without hesitation that I would not have survived the loss of Sarah without her. I know it, as sure as I know my name. She is my hero.

May 19

Went into a Christmas store. They had a big tree decorated in purple and blue (Sarah's and Emily's favorite colors). As we were walking out, there was this stone angel about three feet tall. The sun was shining right through a sun catcher wind chime that was reflecting a blotch of purple right on her chest. Even miles from home, she is everywhere. And I am lonesome for her.

Larry bought Emily a geode to crack open at T-Rex at Legends in Kansas City. It was a pretty cool experience for her. When she cracked it open with the lever machine, it made a huge *pop,* and everyone standing around was amazed. It fell open and revealed the most beautiful inside with amazing shades of blue. Chanda bought her a purple-stone necklace on a blue string. It has been a great day.

May 25

Joel Osteen just said that we should not put a question mark where God has put a period. That will be my biggest shortcoming as Sarah's mom.

May 29

Bad, bad, very bad night.

May 30

Things always look better in the light of day.

June 2

:(Baby shower today. With everything, Sarah is not here.

June 5

Any critical loss robs us of something primary and necessary to whom we are fundamentally. I don't know where to go with grief but to God. Even then, there are days in which I have to be very still to hear Him; sometimes the sadness is just too loud.

June 7

OMGoodness!

The woman on the news just said, "Good afternoon. It is September 23 . . . oh, what am I saying? It is June 7!"

I about fell out of my chair. I have been thinking off and on about Sarah and Cambree all morning, wondering if they know I love them a *whole bunch*. And then that newscaster says the wrong date, and it just happens to be the day we lost Sarah and the day that Cambree is due.

Amazing.

June 8

Here us the thing about grief: when I don't have anything I *have* to do, I do nothing. I sit and think about Sarah. Thankfully, my mom and daughters will not leave me alone. So today I am dressed and going shopping.

Going to see Sarah.

Getting in the pool. Forgetting it all. The bank. Sarah's missing flowers. My broken flip-flop. All of it is floating away.

Southern blueberry cobbler ice cream and the swimming pool. Take that, society.

June 10

Can I just tell you that the Big G (grief) sneaks up on people when they are not looking and whips them but good? I thought I was doing pretty good. Turns out I am not.

I have again started the really weird phenomenon that I encountered in the first week after Sarah died. My body is back into a very primitive mode. Not eating at all until I am starving. Not sleeping at all until I am exhausted and then dropping off to sleep in short durations. There is no real pleasure in food or cooking, just eating to survive. There is no real rest, just my body rebooting. I don't always eat at mealtime. And I don't always sleep at night.

Nine months ago, I would have never guessed that there was this physical side to the Big G. I always thought it was a mental, spiritual, and emotional punch. Turns out I have quite a bit of achiness and muscle weakness.

We have developed a schedule so that I have something to do every day that requires me getting dressed and leaving the house. Today Emily and I went to the flea market and bought some wooden pieces that she is going to paint. Tomorrow we are going to buy a corned beef roast to cook. And I don't know what we are doing on Tuesday.

Emily and Mom and Caroline have been just a bit insistent about me getting better. In fact, they have been downright bitchy about it. It always seems that when one of us is a wreck, the other women pick us up.

Thankfully, we haven't all crashed at the same time. It is a strong tribe of women that I call mine. Cambree will be well served by being born into this heritage of strength; it will carry her through when she is weak.

June 11

I couldn't see my doctor today, and because Mom was very insistent that I see someone today, we went to urgent care. Ironically, the PA who was my health care provider lost her daughter unexpectedly in October. She knew *exactly* what I couldn't articulate. Hopeful.

June 12

I am doing so much better today. And again I am without words as to how a person gets through something difficult without friends and family.

The last two weeks have been hell, but the last twenty-four hours have been miraculous. I was amazed that God worked it out so I could have the physician I had yesterday. Spencer is swimming with me, showing me his new skills, looking up from the pool to see my brother, who I haven't seen since Christmas. I had a meal out with Mom, my brother, and the kids and an empty chair—literally a chair was randomly left empty beside me. I was choked up when I noticed it. And a visit to Sarah's grave and Dad's grave. A good night's sleep. A friend bearing coffee this morning. My girls helping me clean house today. And a nice, hot shower.

My head is clearer now than it has been in a while. Dad used to say I have places to go and people to see. Someone else used to say I have people to do and places to see.

I have work to complete and a mission to get to.

June 14

I am feeling better and better. I got some things taken care of today. Not big things, just things that I have been letting others take care of for me for a couple of weeks—cleaning a bit, mowing lawn, running errands. There is something about taking care of myself that makes me stronger.

It is a vicious cycle. I feel bad, so I don't want to do anything, so I feel worse, so I do less. It is hard to dig my way out of that Big G hole. Blessed am I, for I have someone who made me do a small thing so that I could do more the following day and even more the next day. And finally I was able to mow the yard and go to the grocery store myself.

It is a good thing. It is a good day. It is a good life.

June 15

Guess what. Today is the day. I feel 100 percent like my old self (my old self since losing Sarah). I finally think I am going to make it. Thank goodness for loved ones and medical intervention. I am thinking positively and creatively again. I miss her with everything I have, *but* today I can miss her and still be thankful for my life. A few days ago I couldn't do that.

June 17

Emily is going to see Sarah. She got her some flowers from Hobby Lobby that hang down. She wants to add them to Sarah's vase. I am not getting out of the car. I have done really well the last couple of days and don't want to move backward.

June 22

Driving around with Emily, listening to "Imagine." Sarah sang that song three times that morning on the way to school. She was the best brown-eyed pussycat.

June 23

Nine months—the amount of time it took to bring her into this world. I wish I could deliver my grief into another world, but it is getting more bearable.

Today was a day of *epic* failure for our family. It has been nine months today since we lost Sarah, and the only explanation for the chicanery of today is that Sarah has messed with us all day.

1. Several weeks ago, I got a new body wash that I *love*! It smells like coconut and is scrubby. So I decided to treat my mom to a bottle of it. I took it to her, and she instantly opened it and started rubbing it on her arms. I say, "Hey hey hey! What are you doing? That is not lotion. It's body wash." I swear, I wonder about her sometimes.
2. Larry and I went to Lowe's today and as we were parking *he hit the light pole*. It was one of the poles that has a big cement base, and he couldn't see it from the driver's seat. When he did it, he said, "Emily! Watch out for that pole!" (She wasn't even with us). Blame it on the kids; that's how he rolls.
3. I made Mitch's favorite (strawberries with sugar and bananas) for our cookout this evening. He was *so* very excited. He made his plate and sat down and started eating. He said, "I have one question for you. What is in that little glass bowl?"

I said, "Salt."

He said, "Oh, probably wasn't meant for the strawberries."

No, it wasn't.

So a special thanks to our angel for this hilarious day. We loved and enjoyed each other and missed you as we always do. Today was a good day.

June 24

Mom is cleaning out Sarah's room today and packing up some things. I have wanted it done, but couldn't do it myself and couldn't ask anyone else to do it. I don't know how Mom knew I wanted it done, but I am so thankful she has the love and strength to do it. I cannot be in the room *at all*, and it is weird to hear someone thumping around up there, but we are going to leave her door open from now on.

July 2

At the store earlier this week, someone asked me how Sarah was doing. They had no idea that she had died. When I told her, she instantly welled up and cried right in Hobby Lobby.

Last night, I found some pictures on the Internet of Sarah that were beautiful. I had never seen those pictures before, so it was like a little visit from her. And as with any little visit with a loved one, it didn't last long enough.

In addition, I have had two dreams about her in the last twenty-four hours. In one, I was looking everywhere for her, and my dad came to me and asked me, "Don't you know where she is? Don't you know she is fine?" Then he hugged me, and I could smell him. You know that smell that filled your childhood home? The smell of safety and cooking and clean sheets and autumn when you turn on the heater and it burns off the summer dust?

In the second dream, I was in a line to get in to a place to see Sarah. She came up behind me and startled me and then laughed. She looked great. Her eyes were happy, and she had that easy smile. She was dressed just like everyone else, in light blue. She asked me if I knew why she was in this place. I told her no, and she just laughed. She told me that she had gone ahead of us to get it all ready. I told her that now that I knew where she was, I would bring her some stuff and come visit. She told me that she didn't need any stuff and that I couldn't come and visit, but she would visit me. And then she was gone. Again, I didn't hear her voice, just the message, and I didn't get to hug her.

So all of these emotional events led to a big old crying jag last night. It was one of those with the body-wracking sobs. It was one of the worst that I have had in a long, long time. I always associate the breeze on my face with Sarah, but as I was sitting there, the breeze blew across my back (which had been achy from the tension). How cool is that?

Emily came out, and we sat together and cried and talked for a while. I told her about the breeze thing and how I always associated the breeze with Sarah. After a while, I told Emily that I thought we were going to be okay. Right at that instant, a big, chilly gust of air came up and blew for the longest moment and then died down.

Perhaps it was just a coincidence. Perhaps it was just the weather. But maybe it was Sarah telling us that we are going to be okay. One thing I know is that the essence of her love is still around, and we are comforted by it.

Is it as good as the real thing? No. But it is as much as we can ask until we see her again.

July 4

Arrived for our first Freedom Celebration at the lake without Sarah. Mitch and Caroline had saved us a spot that was different from our usual spot, and I fixed different foods. When we pulled up, we thought it was a pretty good spot—in fact, Larry got out and said, "Yep, this is a good spot," and bent down and picked up a purple flower on the ground.

July 9

Larry and I have been married for nine years today. He took on three girls who were not yet teenagers and has borne the financial and emotional responsibility for their raising. He has attended ball games and pig shows, bought school supplies and school clothes, helped pay for a wedding, college, school lunches, and a funeral. He has made sure that they had reliable vehicles and shot them gas money. He has bought pink bedspreads and painted a bedroom purple. He has had little girls crawl in bed with us during thunderstorms, nightmares, and heartbreaks. He took us all to the Grand Canyon,

Mesa Verde, and Las Vegas. He has made fun of boyfriends, bathing suits, and hair styles. In addition to a husband, nine years ago today, I got a co-parent. When he asked me to marry him, he told me he would be a positive influence in the lives of my daughters. He was right.

July 10

Guess who put on makeup today.

Guess who got out of the house not once but twice today.

Guess who sat down and relaxed away from home today.

Guess who didn't panic when there was an unexpected knock at the door today.

Guess who didn't cry one time today.

ME!

July 27

Well, after praying and crying for one hour, we have been able to reach Emily. I knew where she was and who she was with, but I just couldn't reach her. Texted and called and called and texted. They were just in a zone where they could not get any service.

I am so thankful that I have good friends like Lane and Coach Hutchinson, who helped me through this tough evening. *And* Mitch and Caroline, who got to see the entire ugly, hot mess. Fortunately she was with a really trustworthy friend, or I would have probably had to have been institutionalized.

After not drinking soda for twelve days, I have set my new goal. Here is the next thing I am working on: not being a paranoid nutcase.

July 28

Had a very nice visit with some of Sarah's and Emily's friends today.

I am used to my house being full of teenagers. As a group, they are pretty friendly, loud, clumsy, and good people. In and out and eating and swimming and sitting on the front porch and wanting freedom and keys and money and to be cool. What I never knew was what unique and loving people they were as individuals. Today we have been reminded that Sarah found and brought out the best in people. I am going to start doing that. Finding the best in people.

July 29

Stupid nightmares.

I was thinking of when she was in the hospital with her blood clot. She was so kind to the staff. Even though she was miserable, she still woke up for her treatments and asked questions. She wrote a paper about her experience.

I have a picture on my phone of her eating chocolate cake after her MRI in Claremore. It was the first time she had felt well enough to eat.

Instead of going to the church to plan a wedding, I went to plan her funeral.

Instead of a car, I bought her a coffin.

Instead of a prom dress, I bought her clothes to be buried in.

Instead of college, I paid for a headstone.

I thought of her hair today. It was so thick and had so much body. I loved to brush it and French braid it. It had started to fall out a bit because of some of the medication she had been on. But she still had the best hair out of all of us.

I was thinking today that I had wanted her to graduate from Blackwell, because they have such good class reunions. Guess that doesn't matter now. She will never take her babies back to show them where she went to school or where she played as a child.

On the last trip to Tulsa to the doctor, she wanted to drive by her dad's house, and we did. We looked for her grandparents' house, but couldn't remember where it was.

August 3

Tonight I was out in the pool, and Larry stood outside the pool, talking to me. Caroline and Mitch were setting at the outside table. Emily was inside cooking supper (she is the best cook). It was so relaxing.

Then as I got into the shower, I was thinking of what she would be doing if she were here. She would have given Mitch some smack and after Larry, Caroline, and Mitch had gone in, she would have sat on the top step and said she didn't really want to swim, but wanted to talk to me.

We would have chatted, and eventually she would have taken off her shirt and jumped into the pool in her shorts and bra. I loved the look of peace she would have on her face when she tipped her head back into the water to get it wet.

Then we would come into the house, and she would turn up her nose at whatever we were eating and have an apple—unless we were having meatloaf.

It doesn't matter how good it is, there will always be that empty place in our house, that silence where there used to be murmuring, that calmness where there used to be insanity.

But for a new normal, this evening was a good evening.

August 5

Well, today wouldn't have been complete if we didn't get a little nudge from Pussycat.

At the end of the swimming season, when we close our pool, we don't drain it; we just chemical it up and cover it. In the spring, we drain it down real low, fill it back up, run the filter like crazy, and away we go. So the pool has not been completely drained in a long time.

I was spending some time alone in the pool this evening (often where I go to think about Sarah). I was cleaning and scrubbing the bottom with the broom, and when I got finished, I decided to clean out the filter. As I pulled the hose off, I noticed a needle go down the tube. So I drained the tube over my hand and sifted through the leaves. There was what I had first thought was a needle. Turns out it was a gauge.

Later I asked Emily whether or not any of the kids lost a gauge in the pool the last time they were all there. She said, "What does it look like?" I told her that is was small and silver. She got a very odd look on her face and said quietly, "It was Sarah's. She lost it in the pool last year, and we never could find it." After looking at it, she deemed that it was in fact the lost and searched-for gauge.

I have to tell you that I am amazed at how present Sarah still is. Part of us lingers long after we are gone, and that is a comforting thing.

August 6

On what would have been Sarah seventeenth birthday, we bought her a headstone. On what would have been the day that she enrolled for her senior year, we opened a memorial scholarship account. And both of those things are just really yucky.

But some really incredible things happened on those days too. We visited with people that we love a lot. We were lifted in prayer. We felt our baby move. We cooked and enjoyed kitchen time. We talked. We laughed.

We miss her so much. But we are so blessed.

August 8

Caroline is having bad dreams about Cambree. I hate that for her. I think my daughter has developed a mother's worrying heart. I really wish that Sarah had her school clothes laid out for tomorrow and was lying awake wondering what the first day of her senior year would be like.

August 9

Caroline put me in the best frame of mind. She said that Sarah was enjoying her first day as a senior in heaven.

I cannot allow myself to even consider what today would be like if she were here.

August 14

I am so thankful for what remains and for what will come.

I had the weirdest dream within a dream last night. I dreamed that I was dreaming Sarah had died. In the dream, I woke up, and it had all been a nightmare, and she was still here. I was so relieved—you know, that feeling when you wake up and realize that you had just been having a nightmare.

I think I dreamed this because, the other day, while blowing my hair dry, I had my head turned upside down and Emily walked by. Such a normal, simple morning, and I thought, *What if this was the most colossal nightmare ever, and I am going to wake up and she will be here.*

In the dream I just kept hugging her and crying in relief that it had all been a dream. It was not fun to wake up and realize that she was really gone. I guess that part of the drudgery of long-term grief is that we reach the point that the numbness wears off and we are left with a reality that we never wake up from.

When she died, her comforter was in the laundry, and after it was washed I never put it back in her room. Just folded it up and put it away. And since she died, I have slept in my room once. There has been a feeling that if I allow things to go back to normal, it will be admitting that I am okay with the fact that she is gone. And while I have peace, I will never be okay with her not being right here.

Tonight, as I was putting up some laundry, I stumbled upon the comforter. It doesn't smell like her, but it does smell like my home. It is black on one side and white with large black flowers on the other. It wasn't exactly what she had in mind when we ordered it, but when it came in, she loved the texture. She would often pull it off her bed and wrap up in it on the couch.

Something about that comforter gave me whatever I needed to sleep in my own bed. So for the second time in eleven months, here I am snuggled up in my own bed—but this time in her comforter. The texture is really different. It is cotton, but it is very soft and stays cool.

I have spent most of my life valuing people instead of things. So it is very strange that I find myself getting comfort from her things—especially since she didn't value "stuff" either. I really don't understand myself much anymore.

But there is one thing that I do understand. It may be the only thing that matters. I understand love.

August 15

I found my old bucket list from January 2011 and compared it to my current one. I was struck by the fact that I have completed more on my current list than I did on my old one. I guess that losing Sarah has motivated me to do things I wouldn't have before.

There were three similarities in the two lists. So I guess I will be traveling to Alaska, singing karaoke one time, and trying to pass the Art test this year.

I am going to do every cool thing that she never got to do, so I can tell her all about one day.

I slept so good. Lots of dreams that she was still alive. I would be hugging her close and look down, and it would be Caroline or Emily or Mitch.

More than feeling her love for me, I miss showing her my love for her; at least that is how it has been recently.

Regardless, I feel a bit rejuvenated this morning. Quiet and melancholy but rejuvenated.

August 16

Well, guess who slept in her big-girl bed again last night. I dreamed all night long. Last night, the feature playing in my head starred the girls and me. Caroline and I were walking, and I was carrying Emily and Sarah. I liked down, and Emily was crying. I had dropped Sarah, and I couldn't find her.

I always wonder how much connection that there is between dreams and reality. Emily cried hard last night. She also cried a lot in my dreams.

I still feel more rested than I have in a while. There is something about sleeping in my bed that gives the loss more permanence.

I read yesterday of teens killed in car accident in Payne county. I was so physically ill thinking of their families that I thought I would vomit. All that brilliance and hope and companionship is just gone.

I wish that I could convey to their families what I didn't know when Sarah first died, that I know now: while so much is gone, the love remains.

August 21

In the end of *The Perfect Storm*, Mark Walberg says "Skip, I think we're gonna make it." George Clooney's character replies with resignation, "She's not gonna let us out."

That is where I am today. Yesterday and today, I have barely had my head above water. At school, at home, in dreams, I am drowning in missing Sarah. I think that I am going to finally be able to swim my way out, and by the time I get home, I realize I am no closer to shore than I was almost eleven months ago.

I am like a buoy that is not moving, just bobbing in the water.

The sadness and grief is never going to let me out. While I am so blessed and aware every day of the simple and good and decent things and events of my life and have happiness, I don't think I will ever feel true joy again.

August 23

I have said this before: Some days it is easier to miss her than it was to worry about her. Today was not one of those days.

August 26

I dreamed about her last night. I was checking on Emily and Caroline in their rooms. Sarah's bedroom door was closed, and I opened it just to go in and sit with her things for a while. When I opened the door, she was there! I ran to the bed she was sitting on and knelt beside her. I was crying, and she took my face in her hands and wiped my tears with her thumbs. She smiled a knowing, sympathetic smile. But she didn't say anything.

August 28

She would also love that I opened the door to her bedroom tonight and left it open. I didn't go in and sit, but it is open.

September 1

Worked myself up to a really big fit Thursday.

I was very upset before the game, as the night felt like the night Sarah died. The night she died, I had made a quick trip home to pick up Larry and then back for the game. It had been an exciting day and beautiful evening. As we were going to the game that night, Larry had mentioned how bright Venus was, and we spent a lot of time looking at it while watching the game from the end zone.

This past Thursday night, the situations were very similar—the temperature, the excitement, a quick run home, and looking at the sky for the blue moon.

I worked in the concession stand Thursday night. We were slammed busy. The radio station gave free hotdogs and bottles of water, and because it was an old rivalry, the stands were full. It was my first time to run the stand by myself, and it was chaotic at best. An adult from the other team's fan crowd called a student who was working in the concession stand a "little faggot," and another one told me that I "sucked." The student was so upset, and I was upset for him. It was ridiculously cruel.

As we were leaving, it occurred to me that I was starving, and while sitting in the line at a fast-food drive-through, I knew that I had reached that point.

After we got home, I went out onto the patio (where I go to cry for Sarah), and Luke and Rachel (who have gotten used to these random late-night crying jags) assumed their position of comforters—one on each side. After a while of crying, I noticed that my body was really hurting, so I lay down on the ground, and Luke *really* did not like that. He whined and paced and went to the door, trying to get Larry, and then he lay on me for a while. I wonder if he remembers that first night when I lay in the back yard screaming for Sarah.

The episodic crying has really been something to get used to, as I was not a crier before Sarah died. I will be fine for days or even a couple of weeks at a time, and then I crash and burn. The big jags are getting fewer and further apart, but perhaps because they are less frequent, they are bigger.

Another really strange thing is that after one of these big crying fits, I am physically exhausted and achy. It is what I imagine an athlete's body must feel like after a contest. I was so sore and tender yesterday, and my head hurt, and I was tired and weak. But my heart felt some relief.

After our meeting at school yesterday, I came home and crashed. I slept all afternoon, was up for a couple of hours, and then back to bed for the night.

Now I will be fine for a couple of weeks. So today I did some things that I typically enjoy.

I haven't done a lot of cooking since Sarah died. It is a combination of just being bored with cooking and not motivated and physically not having the energy to do it. So yesterday I made a menu of some recipes I want to try and a grocery list. I went to the store and, with my list in hand, made some plans.

Tonight I tried out the first of several new recipes, and it was a hit. I also printed off the music for a new song that has been haunting me, and I worked it up on the piano. One of my students inspired me to get back to work at music. It is such a primal part of me. I think it will be therapeutic for me to get serious about it again. I also had Spencer (who totally cracks me up). His new word is *perfect*.

It still amazes me that after so much is grieved out of me, there is still so much of me that remains. I don't think I will ever get over it, but I think I will find a way to live with it.

September 2

I have come to realize that in the days following a big crying fit, I am more myself than at any other time. It is truly a removal of the cobwebs of grief with one big broom's sweep.

Such a relief.

September 10

Here is my rant. I took Emily to a doctor to get her something to help her sleep. We have tried over-the-counter medication, which has been effective in the past. However, September is proving to be a little tough on us—a little more so than we expected, as we have been doing relatively well. I told him that she was struggling with sleep and crying a lot, and the other issues she has been having. I told him we had tried other things, and I felt it was time for her to have some medical assistance in the form of antidepressants.

This was his response:

> Emily, you just need to change the way you think. Change the way your brain works [he made mechanical sounds with his hands at his head and his fingers wiggling]. You just need to remember the happy times and forget the sad parts. Everyone goes through this. Emily, look at me. Everyone loses someone, and you just have to go on and take care of yourself. If I put you on antidepressants at fifteen, where will you be at thirty? Your sister would not be proud of how you are acting. I will not put you on antidepressants. I am going to write you a prescription for Valium.

I was floored. This is a respected doctor in this town who apparently knows nothing about clinical depression.

1. A person cannot be told to change the way her brain works any more than a person with heart disease can be told to change the way her heart works. The fact that a professional said these words speaks volumes about why the mentally ill often go untreated in this world.
2. Really? Did we need the sound effects?
3. We do remember the happy times. That is what makes our situation so painful. We know that even though we do have happy times now and will continue to find happiness, we will *never* again share that happiness with Sarah or hear her laugh or see her smile. We don't think about the sad parts. We honor her and love her and remember her and pine for her.
4. No, everyone has not gone through it. Emily is the only Emily Jane Ray who ever lost a Sarah Virginia Ray. Every situation of grief and critical loss is different. There may be similarities with situations and the process of grief, but if someone says to me that they know how I feel, I instantly know that they do not. If they did, they would never say that.
5. How dare he talk to a fifteen-year-old like she is a child? She has grown and experienced and functioned and floundered and soared through a tremendous amount of shit in the last year. And if she wants to hang her head when her suffering is being belittled and discounted, I think she is allowed.
6. If he puts her on antidepressants at fifteen, what will she be when she is thirty? Probably a functioning adult like her mother. I have been on antidepressants for over fifteen years. In those fifteen years I have gone to college, taught a ton of kids, raised three great daughters, been a good daughter and sister and wife, cooked some amazing things, drawn some pretty cool doodles, and learned to fire a gun. What I have *not* done in the past fifteen years is hurt myself or others, self-medicate, become a shell of a person, or end my life. My clinical depression was probably hereditary, as was my mother's and a few relatives' *and* Emily's. I am not even 100 percent sure hers is related to Sarah's death. In fact, given the fact that Emily had a sister with serious self-worth and

depressive tendencies, I tend to think that this would have developed in Emily sooner or later regardless.

7. Valium? Really?
8. And finally, and I want to be absolutely clear about this, Sarah would be proud as punch at the tremendous job that Emily is doing. She would be proud of all of us. Sarah knew the depth of love that existed in this house. We all did. And we all knew how at any moment it could be taken away, and the loss would have devastated everyone left behind. Sarah would want Emily to know that she is showing a strength that she herself would have not been able to. And I want Emily to know that she is my hero.

September 11

I realize on this national anniversary that the events of my life (my brother being deployed so many times, the death of my daughter) have made me much more aware of the humanity and beauty of love and patriotism, and of the futility and briefness and permanence of life. Happy things, sad things, heartfelt things, genuine things. These are the things that make me cry. On the flip side, I am much less patient with people who are not genuine and are careless with their emotions.

September 12

I am now in a classroom that she has never hung in after school. I have never seen her come slopping into this classroom and slop her bag down in the middle of the floor and raid the fridge and happy bucket. I have never seen her asleep on this classroom floor or found her surfing on the pull-down menu of my computer. I haven't typed a paper for her during her senior year.

A new little person is coming who she will never hold or feed or rock in her rocking chair. One sister is turning into a mother; the other has gotten her permit and will become an aunt.

Her mother learned to shoot a gun, came across some books and quotes that she would like, and took everything out of the cabinets in the kitchen to clean the cabinets tonight and left everything spread out when she got tired (she would find this typical and funny).

Some people and events would have left her surprised, disappointed, impressed, and/or provoked. Things have been imagined, dreamed, and dreaded that she probably imagined, dreamed, or dreaded before all of us.

She has missed some awesome things, but not nearly the awesomeness of what we have missed.

September 16

So proud of Caroline. Once she got her hips realigned and antibiotics, she has relaxed and is enjoying these last few days of being pregnant. We really thought that all of the pain she was in and how lousy she was feeling was because she was thirty-eight weeks pregnant. Turns out, she didn't know how bad she was until she was better. She is in the home stretch. One more week until Cambree's due date and the anniversary of Sarah earning her wings. My heart is full.

Several years ago, I was at the fair with a friend, and Sarah and Emily were with their friends. I felt a strong need to talk to Sarah, and I called on her cell phone. I couldn't get her, and I kept trying and trying. The feeling that I needed to touch base with her was very pressing, so I went to the home of the friend she was staying the night with. She was drunk. I was pissed. As I helped her to the vehicle to haul her home, she leaned on me and whispered in my ear, "I'm so sorry, Mom. I'm so sorry I disappointed you."

Tonight as we parked to go to the fair, I looked up, and we were parked right in front of that house with the mailbox I had to maneuver her around on that night.

I thought about her so much tonight at the fair. I almost cried as we watched the younger kids on the swings. I remembered how she would throw her head back and close her eyes and hold her arms out. The swings made her feel so free. I walked away.

There was a mom putting her three daughters on a ride. They were all laughing and having such a sweet time together. I remember that sweet time when they were all three young and we were so happy. Simple.

I bought a caramel apple. She and I always split one, so I had to throw part of it away. But even though I thought of her and wished she was there to share it with me, I wasn't too emotional about that part.

It is funny how sounds and noises and smells, bring back memories as much as sights do. Seems like all evening I thought, *This time last year, we . . .*

Soon a day will pass. After that day, I will not be able to say, "Last year she was still here."

She is getting further away. I do not want her to be part of my past. I do not want to lose her presence. I do not want to get used to her being gone.

However, no matter how beautiful the penmanship, there is always a little smudge on the paper. We have some really great times, but the fact remains that no matter how good those times, she is not there to share them with us, and we are always cognizant of that.

September 17

I remember things that I thought in those first few days. I was so bothered by the fact that people referred to her as an angel. I don't know why, but I was adamant about looking it up and proving to myself, if no one else, that she was a dead human not an angel.

Angels and humans have different roles in heaven and are not interchangeable.

I also remember thinking that kids had nowhere to go with grief and really no way to cope with it. Even as adults, we do not know how to help them. I think that we do a disservice to our kids when we shelter them from grief and loss. Many children who didn't know Sarah were grief stricken due to fear of the unknown and lack of experience with grief. If Grandpa or Grandma passes, I think we should let the children be part of the process.

I went to see Sarah today and cried for an hour, asking her if I could please come with her. While I was telling her that I just couldn't do it anymore, there was absolutely no breeze. When I told her that I was trying to find my mission and get to it, there was a strong breeze. It was almost like she was pointing me in the direction in which I should go. After a long time, I got up, brushed off, looked at the back of her headstone, and sang "The Pussycat Song" to her.

I stepped to my dad's nearby grave and noticed that the flowers from his vase were missing. Sarah had some that didn't quite match, so I moved them to his grave. I told him I didn't think she would mind sharing with him. About the time I said that out loud, a huge butterfly came flying out of the flowers in my hand. I told him to make sure she was eating and to make sure she was laughing. I cried over him for a while too.

Then I came home. I ran out to our business to check on Larry and cried a bit there. Went to supper with my kids and Larry, and cried a little bit there when telling Larry about the butterfly. We had come in different cars, and before we drove home in our separate cars, I also cried a little bit when he kissed me and told me he loved me. A friend dropped off a treat for me, and I cried a bit when she left. That is what I have done most of the evening. Cried a bit here and cried a bit there.

Now I am lying in bed eating Cookie Crisp. Turns out that when life kicks the shit out of you, you can eat cereal wherever and whenever you want. And I will tell you something else: I am having some Ruffles tomorrow for supper, and that is all I am having—just chips.

September 19

Today I was told that I was living in the past and that this page is filled with drama. I want to make it very clear that if you feel this way and would not like to read my posts about Sarah, you are free to delete this page. We can still remain friends through my main Facebook page, as I typically do not post about Sarah there.

I use this site as a journal and a place to document that Sarah is not gone from my heart but still affects my life every single day. Some days it causes me to smile, some days . . . not so much.

Grief is a very present thing and is not about living in the past. It is about learning how to live in the now without someone who at one time was critical to my existence.

It has taken a long time to find my way, and I am not certain that I am even on the right path. For the rest of my life, I will walk into a room and expect her to be there. I will hop into the car with my family and recognize that there is no argument about who is riding shotgun. I will notice the empty chair at a table.

Missing my child is not about living in the past, because, until the day I die, I will always, always be Sarah's mom.

September 20

It has been almost a year since I answered the door to two law enforcement officers standing on my front porch, knowing before they said a word that Sarah was gone, beginning our dark descent into a period of great sadness and disbelief. Even still, life is impossible without her insanity. When we released balloons in January for her seventeenth birthday, we all wrote notes to her. Caroline wrote that she wanted to make Sarah an aunt.

A few weeks later, although her child would never know how brown Sarah's eyes were or what a great dancer she was or how her little skinny self could eat a whole watermelon, Caroline was, in fact, going to make Sarah an aunt.

In the spring, we had gone with Caroline for an ultrasound. We were overjoyed to see my baby and to discover that a little girl would be joining us sometime in September. As the technician measured her legs and head, he put the measurements into the computer and it calculated her arrival date to be September 23. It was very quiet in the darkened room as we realized that Sarah was also in the room with us.

While we have always known that the baby will never take the place of our earth child, Sarah, the expectation of her arrival has taken some of the sting out of the approaching anniversary of her leaving us. While we will always wonder what kind of aunt Sarah would have made, we imagine that she would have introduced our little girl to cool music, taught her how to write in cursive, taken her to Sonic for slushes, and given her a place to escape to when she couldn't stand her mom and dad anymore. Sarah would have loved her, protected her, cherished her, and spoiled her. In short, Sarah would have been to this new baby what she was to everyone else—a sweet miracle.

Cambree Danielle Hadley arrived at 9:28 tonight. Sarah was there tonight, because love was there.

September 23

We just got back from the lake. We released seventeen purple star balloons. Each one of them had a word from a loved one on it. There were only enough of us to write on sixteen balloons, so on the last balloon we wrote, "Eagle Pride."

September 27

Stay Fancy Day at DCLA High School. Everyone wore purple. Even purple hair. It was amazing. I am blown away.

September 28

Homecoming night at DCLA High School. It has just recently occurred to me that she went to her home on homecoming. I find irony in that. The loss of her has been rife with irony and little nudges.

At the pep assembly, the kids presented us with an art piece that each one of them had signed. The boys still wear their purple wristbands at every game. We had a huge number of people in the stands in purple. The homecoming candidates wore purple dresses. In the end zone was a sign that said, "Angel in Our End Zone." They released purple balloons at halftime.

After the game, we all went to the dance. Because I am the student council sponsor, I had to be there. I am so glad I went. The kids were so funny and awkward and rhythmic. It is odd to see them out of their normal setting. I am amazed at how everyone is included. It doesn't matter how a person is dressed or who they are, they are a part of this place. It is a rare thing when kids can be themselves even if they are quirky, where it is hip to be kind, and where being an ass is not cool.

It has been a full year, homecoming to homecoming, death to birth, bleakness to brightness. I would have never believed that I could have survived the loss of my child. And I may not still. But I know that today my life is richer than it was on the night that she died. I am stronger. I am kinder. I am more in love with my fellow human beings. I am closer to and more aware of God.

People saved me from being consumed by grief and my own self. A smile here, a card there. A note in the mail, a hot meal, an uplifting phone call. A touch in passing, a cup of coffee when I hadn't been out of bed in a couple of days, an inappropriate joke. My family, my students, my fellow teachers, Sarah and Emily's friends, my own dear friends. I have been blessed with gift of love and acts of kindness from them and from total strangers.

It wasn't until recently that I have come to realize what my meaning of life is. I have always believed that life was about acts of service to others, building relationships, and creating experiences. But now I think it is even simpler than that. The meaning of my life is love. The price I paid for this understanding has been dear, and I do not intend to squander the knowledge.

Love.

R.I.P
Sarah Ray